YO
The Endangered Species

YOUTH
The Endangered Species

MAL FLETCHER

WORD PUBLISHING
Nelson Word Ltd
Milton Keynes, England
WORD AUSTRALIA
Kilsyth, Australia
WORD COMMUNICATIONS LTD
Vancouver, B.C., Canada
STRUIK CHRISTIAN BOOKS (PTY) LTD
Cape Town, South Africa
JOINT DISTRIBUTORS SINGAPORE –
ALBY COMMERCIAL ENTERPRISES PTE LTD
and
CAMPUS CRUSADE, ASIA LTD
CHRISTIAN MARKETING NEW ZEALAND LTD
Havelock North, New Zealand
JENSCO LTD
Hong Kong
SALVATION BOOK CENTRE
Malaysia

YOUTH: The Endangered Species

Acknowledgements

Most of the worthwhile things we achieve in life come as the result of teamwork. Whether or not this book is worthwhile, only time and the reader will tell, but the many people who have contributed deserve praise. I can't thank them all by name, but they'll see their influence in the pages that follow.

Special thanks to: All my colleagues in Youth Alive Australia, for spreading the good news; all at Word Books (Australia), for taking risks; Wendy Moulton for research assistance; Christine McClay for working so hard; Noela Favaloro for being a great typist; Robert McQuillan, for editorial assistance; Harvest Christian Centre and Richmond Assembly of God, Melbourne, for caring; all of my family and the friends I've made in ministry, for your inspiration and kindness.

To my mum and dad: Thanks for giving so much to your kids.

To Deanna, Grant and Jade: I'm so proud of you!

To my long-suffering and encouraging wife, Davina: Thanks for standing by me and helping me to believe in myself. You're the greatest!

Contents

Foreword

If I'd had a few teachers like Mal Fletcher when I was at school, it would have been a much more enjoyable place for me!

As it was, I didn't enjoy myself all that much. I struggled to find a real sense of purpose and identity and, though I dreamed of doing something big with my future, I didn't really believe in myself. Those were unsettled years filled with uncertainties.

With the benefit of hindsight, I can see how God's grace and the concern of caring friends pulled me through. Along the way I became a Christian and I now possess the sense of purpose I lacked as a student. That's why I spend much of my time among young people, offering them a listening ear and a message of hope.

My friend Mal Fletcher shares this burden for the young. In this book he deals with issues which desperately need to be addressed if you and I are to rescue a generation from despair and confusion.

This book is filled with the stark reality of what is happening to a generation of young people today and God's concern for them. It is a book for those who want to learn to understand the pressures young people face and to become practically involved in helping them. You can be part of the answer for young people you care about—if you get involved. This book will give you confidence to reach out and help.

Steve Grace

Preface

Did you ever pray for a thing, and later hope that God didn't hear you?

As a kid, I grew up in a fairly 'straight' home. My parents were committed Christians and they worked hard to keep seven kids on the straight and narrow. It was a fairly protected upbringing in many ways, and for that I'm now grateful. About the most evil thing I could do as a young teenager was wear flares to church! My father thought I was on the skids when one day I brought home a Partridge Family record (Remember them? Totally un-rock 'n' roll: like ABBA on Valium.)

Like all the other kids in my church peer group, I used to pray: 'Lord, show me your will for my life...' I prayed it with feeling, and I really meant it. I wanted to live life to the full, to reach my God-given potential.

But I only half wanted an answer to that prayer. There was one thing I hoped God would not call me to do. I did not want to be a missionary!

You see, when I was a kid, missionaries were considered very uncool. They came to your church once a year, dressed in safari suits (very bad for the image) and showed slides of the Congo, for at least an hour at a time. These were the people to whom some church folks mailed their used teabags! Each Christmas, we collected all our unwanted used toys and sent them to the missionaries' children. Every year they received parcels full of cars without wheels and dolls without heads. Being a missionary was not something I aspired to. I decided that there were a lot more comfortable ways to see the world.

Of course, over the years, my opinion of missionaries improved a great deal, but I can't honestly say that I ever wanted to become one.

Then one day, not too long ago, my eldest daughter and I had an interesting discussion. She asked me why I was always going out to speak to groups of young people. I told her that this was part of my job, but before I could of touch fully explain she dropped the bombshell.

'Daddy,' she said, looking up at me, innocently, 'Would you say that you're a kind of missionary? Gulp! I realised at that moment, that the very thing I had spent most of my life avoiding, I have now embraced. I am a missionary.

I, and many others like me, talk to young people all over this country, week in and week out, about the problems and issues which concern them most. Their world seems so very different from the one in which I spent my teenage years. The streetscape of their lives is foreign to many adults, who grew up in less confusing, if not easier, times. They are being forced to confront issues and answer questions which were unheard of a generation ago.

Many modern young people live in a state of moral confusion. They live in the most rapidly changing society in history. For some, the pace of change is far too rapid and, when they can't make sense of it all, they opt out of life in one way or another. Australia, the so-called 'lucky' country, now has the highest rate of youth suicide in the world.

We all have young friends, peers, or children whom

we want to help. Like all the very best missionaries throughout history, we must make every effort to discover the perceived and real needs expressed in this 'foreign culture' of theirs. Then we must work to meet those needs.

I have spoken with thousands of parents and friends of distressed youth, who desperately want to offer hope and practical assistance to the young. Yet so many feel incompetent and ineffectual in reaching out to young people. Basically, they lack confidence and they feel out of touch.

The first half of this book describes some of the unique questions the youth of today are facing. The second half offers practical principles which, if applied in relationships, will assist in building bridges of communication between you and the young people you care for. I have also included a section dealing with severe or suicidal depression and, finally, a number of practical communication exercises which may help restore understanding where it has broken down.

I hope this book comes as both an encouragement and a challenge to you. My deepest wish is that, after reading the chapters which follow, you will find in your heart a deeper compassion for the young, an expanded awareness of the pressures they face, a greater empathy for their feelings and hurts, and more binding commitment to help them.

As one youth missionary to another, I wish you God's wisdom—and His undying patience.

Mal Fletcher

Part One

Whatever Happened To Innocence?

CHILDREN DYING

twilight
the city lights
burn in her eyes.
she stumbles,
recovers,
she quietly cries . . .

childhood reflections
flash by
in her mind:
the few caring moments
she's known in her
    time . . .

alone
in the darkness,
she stares at the floor;
wondering just why
she has come back for
    more . . .

inside
she trembles
she waits for the high;

she empties the needle
and wishes to die . . .

out in the suburbs
alone
in his room,
stereo blaring -
a soul-chilling tune;

he pauses
to wonder
just why he was born,
when fifteen years later
he's ending it all . . .

children crying,
does anybody hear?

children dying
does anybody care!?

Mal Fletcher

1

Where Have All The Families Gone?

The Death Of An Institution

Some authorities claim that the greatest cause of depression among young people is trouble within the family unit—especially discord between parents.

One unfortunate by-product of the Industrial Revolution was the breakdown of the extended family. Men began to move away from their traditional homes, taking their own families with them in search of work in the new industrialised cities. Grandparents, aunts and uncles began to play a far lesser role in the development of the child than they had previously. A very important social network began to be taken from the child.

More recently, the 1960s brought what some chose to call the 'sexual revolution'. This time it was the nuclear family that was to suffer. Sexual experimentation outside the marriage bond has broken the back of thousands of marriages, devastating the lives of hundreds of thousands of children at the same time.

Our divorce rate tripled in eight years during the late 1970s. Currently, 900 couples split up each week. Divorce costs taxpayers £0.7 billion per year—that's

£215 per family. About 750,000 children now live in families where one or both parents have remarried and, if divorce rates continue at current levels, more than a third of first marriages will end in divorce.[1]

About 40% of remarriages will end in divorce, and many children will go through the pain of more than one family breakdown. Around 16.5% of children will see their parents divorce by the time they are 16 years of age.[2]

There are a number of factors which place strains on family relationships. High levels of unemployment and declines in real wages; smaller families where more is invested in and then expected from each member; the tendency for children to remain in school and at home longer; and the increasing rate of change in society, change which can seem to make parents irrelevant to the world of their children. All these have their negative affect.

In The Wake Of Tragedy

Sadly, so much is said and written about the rights of the marriage partners in a family split that the responsibilities of parents to their children often seem to rate a distant second in priority.

One Institute of Family Studies research paper stated that almost half of the children surveyed in the 8–9 years age group feared that their parents might separate. One third of those surveyed in the 15–16 years age bracket were afraid of a marital split between their parents.[3] Family tensions and divorce leave a permanent impression on the teenager or child in the home and can even become major contributing factors to depression.

Social alienation among young people, say some experts, stems from their sense of not belonging to any of the 'four worlds of childhood': family, school, work and friends. In days gone by, someone who suffered in one of these areas could normally find security and comfort in the others. Now, many young people feel estranged from several of these worlds at the same time. As a result, they suffer sustained social alienation.

Emile Durkheim, the French social scientist of the nineteenth century, was the first to demonstrate that the incidence of suicide in a society was associated with the degree of social integration. He claimed that rising suicide rates resulted from a regression of 'domestic sentiments' and from a loss of 'domestic solidarity'. It is interesting to note that married men and women in all age groups have significantly lower suicide rates than similarly aged single, separated and widowed or divorced persons.[4]

Once upon a time, even if life was uncomfortable in other spheres, at least the family could be relied upon to give some sense of stability. This is no longer guaranteed. Depression in children and adolescents and marital tensions are related in several ways. First of all, it must be noted that young children tend toward egocentricity —that is, they perceive all external events as in some way reflecting on them. For example, if dad and mum are continually arguing, they will come to believe that this is in some way their fault—that they are not a good child. A poor sense of self-worth can set in at a very early age, leaving children particularly vulnerable to feelings of failure as they grow.

An Adelaide child psychiatrist conducted a study into attempted suicide among children aged 14 years and under. He found that suicidal behaviour in that age bracket was most often triggered by depression, family violence, divorce or separation of parents, and recent loss of parents or grandparents through death.

A director of the Australian Institute of Family Studies makes a powerful point: 'Children need close attention from people who care about them as individuals . . . the most caring teacher cannot provide the loving attention of parents or other family members.'[5]

Times of tension in the home are no less traumatic for the adolescent who is grappling with his or her own quest for identity. During periods of marital tension teenagers often feel under pressure to play peacemaker in the home. They may feel manipulated and that they are expected to take sides in the issue or to provide solutions. Thus they are expected to perform a parent-like function, to hold together a highly-stressed relationship between their parents. This sets them up for failure —they are simply not equipped to deal with such problems. As therapists they will fail, adding to guilt and despair.

Another by-product of parental conflict is that teenagers feel robbed of anyone with whom they can share their own very real traumas. Sometimes young people will go to great lengths to gain the attention and empathy they crave. In some cases, attempts of suicide are their way of finding out how much they are loved. They wonder: Would my parents really miss me if I were gone for good? Would they stop fighting long enough to shed a tear for me? This may seem an extreme response, but to a confused child or teenager who does not have the benefit of much past life experience, it is all too often the one chosen.

Children and teenagers are also affected by the economic strains placed on families by divorce and separation. The number of sole parent families grew by a massive 60% in 12 years to reach a total of 320,000 in 1986. A combination of family splits, rising unemployment and price hikes has seen the number of children living in poverty grow dramatically—from 230,000 in 1966 to 800,000 by 1986. By that time about 700,000 households in Australia lacked the means to live above the poverty line. Of these, 400,000 were families with children.[6]

When conflict ends in divorce the children or adolescents also experience a great sense of personal loss, a kind of grief similar to that we feel at the death of a loved one. They face feelings of uncertainty about the future. An integral part of the fabric of their lives—one they assumed would remain intact no matter how great were its conflicts—has now been torn apart. They will be required to adjust emotionally to living away from one or the other of their parents, and to making a whole new world of associations with people and things around them.

Alvin Toffler wrote in *Future Shock* of the 'disease of change' which he said would leave people without roots geographically and relationally in our time.[7] The average family in the West moves house once every three or four years. This is hard enough on children without adding the extra traumas inflicted through marriage breakdown.

Child Abuse
One part of family traumas for too many kids is child abuse.

According to an American study, one out of every three girls and one out of every ten boys are sexually assaulted before the age of eighteen. Experts say there is no reason to believe it is any different in Australia. Some authorities claim that 60% of child sexual assault cases remain unreported. All studies agree on one thing—that the crime normally begins when a child is somewhere between the ages of three and eleven. In fact, by adolescence most of the assaults have stopped. Defenceless children are suffering as a result of this heinous crime.

Child abuse is a major contributing factor to youth suicide. Studies have shown that 65% of all children who are physically abused attempt suicide at some time in their youth. Research has shown that fathers are by far the worst offenders, followed by uncles and brothers. The only female abusers reported are mothers and then only in a very small number of cases.

For some men, small children represent a very attractive sexual alternative to women. Children are, after all, not critical of a man's sexual performance—they do not expect mutuality—and, because they are taught to obey adults, can easily be cajoled into sexual encounters. Many abused children often experience tremendous fear and panic, and most are threatened that if they talk to anyone about the attacks they will not be believed, or they will be punished.

Statistics can be cold and inhuman. We need to look beyond the numbers and see the lives which are traumatised by such attacks. Consider the testimony of 18-year-old Amanda, which was printed in a popular youth magazine as part of an article on incest.

'I can't remember a lot of it. He (her father) would give me drugs, serapax and valium. Sometimes he'd make me drink stuff. Then he'd start kissing me. I really wish there'd been someone there whom I could have said something to. I thought it happened in everyone's family. I didn't know any better . . .

'My mother knew what was going on. I know ... she did but she never said anything. I told her twice—once after I'd tried to OD. I was twelve ... I know I told Mum then what was happening. She never said anything about it ...

'I felt guilty, dirty, degraded. I would spend hours scrubbing myself raw in the shower to try and get rid of the feeling. It's a terrible dirty feeling you just can't get rid of.'[8]

Amanda is one of thousands who all tell a similar story. The result is almost always the same: fears of victimisation set in and future relationships are strained by terrible suspicions. The child victim often carries into adolescence feelings of confusion and guilt and a sense that he or she is somehow unclean and undeserving of affection.

Feelings like these in early adolescence can set the child up for an attitude of despair later on. It is when other perceived failures are built onto this existing base of confusion and low self-esteem, that severe depression can set in.

2

Let's Rage!

Violence Trivialised

Crime has increased over the past few years. Statistics bear this out. Since 1974, for example, the incidence of serious assault has risen by 400%. The number of frauds, robberies and breaking and enters has at least doubled. The incidence of rape has risen by 150%.[1]

Sadly, it is young people who are committing the majority of crimes in most categories. The peak arrest age for crimes against property, for example, is 16 years; for violent crimes it is between 19 and 23 years.[2]

Criminal activity among young people is linked with problems such as illegal drugs, alcohol abuse, unemployment and depression. Studies have shown that depression, especially in boys, often results in feelings of aggression and a desire to hurt people.

Unfortunately, at a time when many young men and women are needing help with violent or aggressive attitudes and behaviour, they are receiving precious little encouragement from the powerful pop-culture media which helps to shape their thinking.

Young people in our society today are constantly being bombarded with scenes of violence in the television programmes and movies they watch, and even in some of the music they listen to. It is no longer only fictional works of violence, for so long depicted in films, which pose a problem; now real violence becomes a part of every day life through television news broadcasts and current affairs reports. Scenes of tortured human bodies and bloodied streets are brought with little real restriction into our living rooms.

The point I wish to make is not that TV, movies or music are solely responsible for increases in violent crime among our youth, but that such a forced familiarity with violence can break down a depressed individual's resistance to aggressive behaviour. Media images which, taken together, can appear to be trivialised and dehumanising violence, may help to push an already stressed young mind over the edge, into the realm where fantasy is lived out in reality.

TV and Movies

Research undertaken by The Australian Children's Television Foundation has suggested that 98% of Australians now live in homes with television sets and that the TV is on for 31 hours per week in the average home. It also revealed that the average child watches TV for 23 hours each week, with one child in five watching more than 40 hours in a week. According to this report, throughout their school lives, children complete 11,500 hours of formal education and in the same period, will view 15,000 hours of television. In that time, it says, they will witness 18,000 murders depicted on TV.[3]

Media people have been known to protest whenever anyone suggests that a link exists between violence

26

depicted on TV or in movies and violent behaviour in real life. The electronic media, they say, simply show life as it is, warts and all, reflecting society's already existing problems.

Unfortunately though, if you reflect a certain type of destructive behaviour often and graphically enough, without any meaningful attempt to discuss its ramifications or to help alleviate it, you may just be reinforcing the presence of that type of behaviour among those viewers who are predisposed to it. Research undertaken, particularly in the United States, has now in fact implicated the media, especially television, in the rising youth suicide rate there.

Television news coverage and fictional movies about suicide often appear to trigger a temporary increase in the number of teenage suicides. Recent findings indicate that sensationalised or romanticised coverage of a suicide may fuel the suicidal tendencies of teenagers.

These findings are consistent with the idea that teenagers are more susceptible than adults to fads, fashion and imitation. Television and films have the ability to romanticise many things for the young—even aggression, death and suicide.

Movies too play a part in promoting violent behaviour. Have you noticed how many celluloid heroes not only experience violence, but find it a necessary part of life? Poor James Bond—he doesn't go looking for violence, it just seems to seek him out and there's very little he can do about it all. Spare a thought for Rambo too, he's really a crusader for justice. He can't avoid slaughter in the battle for right. Violence is a part of life, if you're a hero—it's simply part of the scheme of things.

Without doubt, movies play a part in colouring the whole of a young person's view of life. Movies can appear to cheapen human life even without using graphic depictions of bloody violence.

A concerned mother wrote the following in a letter to a major city newspaper: 'I gave my 10-year-old son £2 spending money. On his return, I asked what sort of day he had. He said that he had watched two naked women mud wrestling and then looked at a man dressed in ladies' stockings, suspenders and underwear. Following that, he had caught up with two unmarried naked teenagers having sex in the back of their car, which was parked in a public car park. He also noticed another two unmarried teenagers go into a parked caravan for the same purpose. '

'. . . The day finished with him learning how to rip off somebody who was buying a second-hand car.

'No, my 10-year-old son doesn't need remedial behavioural therapy. Normally he would not seek out such entertainment. I certainly would not allow these things to be part of his education and if his teacher at school introduced such expressions into his classroom, she would be fired on the spot.'

So how did he get to see all this in a day? Simple: he bought a ticket to see a movie which was rated 'PG' (Parental Guidance recommended).[4]

Music video clips should not go unmentioned either. When was the last time you actually saw a band smile in one of these high-budget, high-tech mini-movies? More often than not the tone of a popular clip is one either of despair or of aggression and aggravation. Often the tense and agitated visual image portrayed has little or nothing to do with the actual song.

Music To Die By

One has to look no further than the names of certain bands to see the influence of violence and aggression in some of today's music. With names such as Violence, Megadeth, Anthrax, Poison and Niggers With Attitudes, who needs to listen to the music backwards to become concerned?

The song and album titles are also gruesome at times. Violence's debut album was called *Eternal Nightmare*. Iron Maiden had a single entitled *The Evil That Men Do*. Slayer has given the world tunes such as *Spill The Blood* and *Mandatory Suicide* while the Misfits sang *Can I Go Out And Kill Tonight*?

In Motley Crue's song Bastard, we hear these words: 'Out go the lights, in goes the knife, pull out his life, consider the bastard dead.'

There are, of course, many songs and groups which blatantly flaunt aggression, and some which go even further to advocate suicide. Bands with names such as Depression and Scraping Foetus off the Wheel (a direct reference to abortion) seem intent on destroying any appreciation of human dignity and personal worth.

Graphically violent or depressing cover art also adds to the image of careless disregard for life. Depression's self-titled album features the most graphically violent cover art I have seen. Most of the cover is taken up with a close-up photograph of a dead black man who has a huge, gaping hole in his forehead, the result of a bullet to the back of the head. The photograph shows only his head and above it, in large white block letters set against a strip of black, is the word 'depression'. That's basically all there is. That will do wonders for the teenager who is already entertaining violent or suicidal thoughts. Another album, entitled *City Baby's Revenge (101 Ways*

29

to Kill a Rat), has on its cover drawings of a baby in nappies holding a hatchet, seven headless rats and a toy dog hanging from a noose. The cover does not belie the contents. Song titles include *Valley of Death, Drugs Party in 526* and *Christianised Cannibals*.

Scraping Foetus Off The Wheel released an album entitled *Hole* on which they had recorded a little tune about death and dying called *Satan Place*. Its lyrics speak of suicide by a gunshot to the head, followed by a journey into hell. *White Knuckles* from the same album contains a similarly morbid suicide theme.

Performers such as these—I will not elevate their status to that of artists—cannot abdicate responsibility for the possible effects of their lyrics on already hurting young people. I could write a book on the subject of music alone —in fact some already have. My purpose here is simply to show how readily accessible these morbid expressions of death are to our teenagers.

George Orwell once described what happens to artists when they find that their work has sunk into the hole of creative mediocrity: 'There is only one escape: into wickedness. Always do the thing that will shock and wound people . . . throw a little boy off a bridge, strike an old doctor across the face with a whip and break his spectacles—or, at any rate, dream about doing such things . . . Along those lines you can always feel yourself original. And after all, it pays!'[5]

Stories such as that of young American John McCollum bear witness to the powerful effect violence-orientated songs can have on troubled young minds.

McCollum was still wearing headphones when his body was discovered in 1984. He had shot himself with his father's .22 calibre pistol, having spent the last few hours of his life listening to heavy metal records. He had

30

been playing two songs repetitively which contained lyrics about suicide. The coroner concluded that McCollum shot himself 'while listening to devil music.' He was only 19 years of age.

Closer to home, a lonely young Melbourne boy aged thirteen took his life in a St. Kilda flat after listening repeatedly to a song called *The End* – a gloom-filled tune about incest and patricide. Young Eben Durrant was considered by some Melbourne clothing designers to be a prodigy. His talent for clothing design led him to start his own label—called *Poor Child*—at the tender age of eleven.

Somewhere along the line he became involved with practising occultists and started keeping knives under his pillow and a hanging rope in his bedroom. He bought morbid books, kept odd company, and played occult games at school. His choice in music did nothing to help this confused boy.

Songs alone cannot be said to cause all suicides. Many factors come into play when a teenager considers ending his or her life. But numbers of psychologists are warning today of the very detrimental affects these forms of songs can have on the already stressed, confused and despairing mind of an unhappy and withdrawn young person.

It's not just the songs which make direct reference to suicide or violence that pose a problem either. Other top 40 releases leave a bitter aftertaste, particularly those which reduce sex to a self-indulgent mechanical act and make relationships into short-lived, physical affairs.

Cartoon Shows

Even the once fairly innocuous TV cartoon show now tends to dish out heavy doses of violent or aggressive behaviour.

Around 1983 a revolution took place in the world of cartoon-making with the birth of shows such as *He-Man*. The hero is known as Adam the Prince of Eternia. When trouble arises Adam points his sword aloft and shouts: 'By the power of Grayskull I have the power!' In actual fact, Adam becomes possessed by the spirit of a demonised castle called Grayskull through an incantation over the sword. Adam's twin sister Adora possesses a similar sword which gives her power to become She-Ra-Princess of Power. She has her own cartoon series which, like He-Man, features an assortment of warlocks and witches.

Other series such as *Ewoks*, *Real Ghost Busters* and *Thundercats* all feature witchcraft and spirit powers of one form or another. Even the *Smurfs* have followed the trend. In one episode, Gargamel, the evil wizard, draws a pentagram on the floor and lights candles at each point. He dances within the pentagram while chanting a spell. A 'magic spirit' enters his body and gives him power to battle the Smurfs. Gargamel did, in front of millions of children, what witches have been doing in dark places through the centuries.

This is an actual ritual of witchcraft. For centuries witchcraft has been denounced by western society. People have, in days gone by, recognised the real evil powers which were at work in the rites of witches, warlocks and the like. Societies recoiled at the cruelty of many of witchcraft's sacrificial rites, banning their practice and driving witches 'underground', thus preventing them from influencing the rest of their community. Parents were anxious to protect their children from such influences. Now, it seems, some people invite aspects of witchcraft into their own homes and allow their kids to vicariously take part in witchcraft practices through identification with cartoon characters.

Should we then be surprised when, as teenagers, some become involved in fantasy role-play games, seances and occultism?

When I attended high school, one of the 'hit' afternoon cartoon shows featured a dog called Scooby-Doo. The story-lines for the show always followed the same simple formula: Some spooky phantom would wreak havoc in a town, driving its people away in droves. Eventually, it would be revealed by Scooby and his friends, avid spook-busters, that the supposed ghost was nothing more than a local evildoer who stood to gain financially through his skulduggery. It was inoffensive light entertainment .

In a more recent episode, the gang were trying to track down a host of demons who had been locked underground for centuries and were now wreaking havoc above ground. What was disturbing to me was not just that demons were part of the story, but that they were depicted for children as physical beings—horrible red creatures with dark eyes, long fingers and horns. Children watching this could be forgiven for thinking that demonic powers are purely a work of fiction. After all, who has ever seen a creature answering that description?

Demonic powers are real. They are not the product of film producers' overly colourful imagination. I have counselled and prayed with people who have suffered great mental anxiety and physical illness because of the influence of evil spiritual forces. Having witnessed what demonic beings do to peoples' lives, it is upsetting to me to see that occult mysticism has found its way even into children's cartoons.

The new breed of cartoon has also given rise to new levels of violence. New weapons have been created for the battle between good and evil. New toys have evolved to allow children at home to act out in play what they learn from watching TV.

Transformers was voted toy of the year in 1985. One study revealed that the associated cartoon series of the same name averages 83 acts of violence each half hour episode. That's almost three acts of violence per minute! Imagine a western with three acts of violence per minute —the action would never move out of the bar-room scene, or away from the shoot-out in the street!

The makers of cartoons such as this one provide our children with opportunity to emulate the violent story-lines of their cartoons. In many instances, the cartoons have simply become half-hour advertisements for ranges of toys based on the characters. Violent scenes are reinforced in children through acting out what they've seen.

There are other violence-related toys and games available now. There is a plethora of Space War Games such as *Master of the Universe* and *Star Scream*. The latter features an introduction which states that: 'Conquest is made of the ashes of one's enemy—for five years and over.'

There are new interactive toys—toys which allow children to shoot at a target on a TV programme and thus to contribute to the final outcome. All of these toys are media-related. The electronic media must accept responsibility for helping to make violence and aggressive behaviour part of our children's everyday life.

Conan & Co.

The print media also play a part in exposing young minds to violent behaviour. Popular newspapers and magazines often feature graphic photographs of blood-ied bodies and war-ravaged streets. Sure, this is life in parts of the real world—but do we need to pick our young people up and carry them to every bloody scene?

Comic books were once dominated by characters such as Superman, Spiderman and the Phantom. A certain amount of pummelling and brawling went on in each issue but some of today's more popular comics make these ageing heroes look positively geriatric when it comes to violence! Consider Conan the Barbarian.

Conan magazine covers feature scantily dressed females in assorted tantalising postures, all drooling over the walking hunk of toughened meat that passes for a Hyborian warrior. Conan is not the most eloquent of men. He communicates basically by muttering inan-ities, grunting a great deal, and swinging your average razor-sharp, javelin-length sword at all and sundry.

You can always tell the characters Conan didn't get along with—they are invariably lying in two halves in a pool of their own blood. In some issues, the drawings are in black and white, but youthful imagination is quite up to the task of filling in the colour—mainly blood red.

The whole back cover will feature advertisements for forthcoming issues, tempting the young reader with some scenes of carnage and bold headlines saying things such as 'Never has so much savagery cost so little!' There's a correspondence page too on which you will find letters from young people, mainly boys, who describe how they really identify with meat-headed Conan. Young admirers can even buy a Conan-style role play game based around battles fought in the Hyborian wars. If the real world is as terrible as our newspapers tell us, why do we need *Conan* comics to make it any worse?

The Games We Play

Aligned with this new breed of cartoon shows and comic books, there are the fantasy role-play (FRP) games such as *Dungeons and Dragons*, *Chivalry and Sorcery* and *Tunnels and Trolls*.

When many of us think of games we remember family *Monopoly* sessions, Scrabble tournaments at school, or grappling with the rules and tactics of chess as beginners. Products such as *Dungeons and Dragons* (*D & D*) are far from the innocent board games of old. On this particular game, Dr. Gary North, author of *None Dare Call It Witchcraft*, comments: '. . . after years of study of the history of occultism, after having researched a book on the subject, and after having consulted with scholars in the field of historical research, I can say with confidence: these games are the most effective, most magnificently packaged, most profitably marketed, most thoroughly researched introduction to the occult in man's recorded history.'[6]

D & D is the most popular of the FRP games and it developed out of the war games of the 1950s. Rather than reconstructing historical or hypothetical conflicts on model battlefields, games like this one are fought in the minds of the players. Each player chooses a role which he or she would like to play, assuming the identity of the character he or she creates. The game is overseen by a Dungeon Master who sets the stage in the fantasy world.

The rules for each game, which can last for hours, days, months or even years, are dictated by the *D & D* manual. Each character will be either 'good' or 'evil' as determined by this book. A person can choose all manner of identities including assassins, magic users, thieves, zombies and druids. One can even play the part of Beelzebub in *D & D*. This is one of the biblical names for Satan.

The game is for three or more players, age 10 and upwards. It is often advertised in the *Conan*-type comics with captions such as 'The Adventure Is Yours With *Dungeons and Dragons*' and '*D & D* opens your world to adventure' or 'Take Your Imagination To A Higher Level.' It is marketed with a sales pitch aimed at young people who hunger for adventure and heroics.

The object of the game is to manoeuvre these characters through a maze of dungeons (tunnels) filled with monsters, magic, ambushes, and adventures in search of treasures. Each character is equipped with weapons ranging from the conventional, such as hand axes, swords and battle axes, to the mystical, such as potions, spells and magical trinkets.

Each player may stay in the game as long as his or her character is not killed.

But *D & D* is much more than a game; it introduces the player to an entire belief system. Referring to deities and gods its handbook says: 'This game lets all your fantasies come true. This is a world where monsters, dragons, good and evil; high priests, fierce demons; and even the gods themselves may enter your character's life.'

What are the deities of the *D & D* fantasy world like? Let's meet a few of them, as they are described in the handbook. Kali (black earth mother) is a goddess the worship of whom requires 'sacrifices of blood, and even an occasional human sacrifice . . . Those sworn to defend her cult will often do so in a sort of berserk, suicidal manner, slaying all who oppose them until they themselves are slain.'

Tlaloc is the rain god. At each full moon, one of his priests must sacrifice a baby or child to him. After the sacrifice, the priest may cook and eat the child.

Tyaa is the winged goddess of evil birds and only women are allowed in her high priesthood. She 'demands the sacrifice of body parts from her more attractive worshippers.'

Aside from the religious connotations of all this talk about demons and magic, there are the possibly damaging affects of the game's morbid fascination with death. We read that death 'is no great matter in most cases, for the character can often be brought back by means of a clerical spell . . .'

Murder is an accepted part of the game. Assassinations are planned and carried out on 'target characters'.

In some parts of the world there are documented cases of young people who have died allegedly as a result of their involvement with *D & D*. Irving Pulling was a 16-year-old student who came home from school one day and committed suicide by shooting himself with a pistol. It is alleged that a few hours before his death he had been involved in a long-running game of *D & D* with other students at his school.

In the course of the game a curse was placed upon his character by another player. His parents contend that this curse placed him under emotional distress. They believe their son concluded that the only way for him to escape the curse was by offering the life of his character as a human sacrifice. Apparently he calculated that if he carried this out his character would have a 97% chance of being resurrected.

Unfortunately, somewhere along the way Irving lost

sight of the distinction between reality and fantasy. The longer a game goes on, the more likely this is to occur, especially with a young person who is already having emotional or psychological problems.

In California, a series of killings which became known as the 'freeway murders' have been linked with *D & D*. Several people, including children, were slain in what appears to have been an 'adventure'. Allegedly, one of the young men responsible for these killings was an obsessive player of the game and, at the age of 21, was so preoccupied with it that it had become his life. His room had been turned into a medieval fantasy world and he often played the game 24 hours a day.

With the hope of gaining real as against imaginary power, he joined a satanic coven and was initiated into Satanism. It has been claimed that he developed a belief in reincarnation while playing *D & D*, and formulated the idea that, if he were to kill people, he would be doing them a favour by sending them to a better place. The real world became part of his game world and people paid for his fantasy with their lives.

Fantasy Addiction

Alongside a growing preoccupation with violence in some areas of the mainstream media and toy industries, we are also witnessing a growth in the pornography industry. Pornographic material is much more accessible to kids now than it ever was to their parents at the same age. Sex is trivialised in pornographic magazines and videos and the links between some pornographic material and violent sex-related crimes are clear in stories such as that of Ted Bundy.

Bundy was a convicted serial killer who confessed to twenty-three murders in the United States and was suspected by police of committing a further eight. All of the victims were women. Hours before his death in the electric chair Bundy was interviewed by psychologist Dr. James Dobson.

Dobson enquired as to the family background of the convicted man, and was told of a fairly average upbringing, without any emotional or physical abuse. How then did Bundy's preoccupation with sex-related violence begin? Let's recall the man's own words:

'. . . as young boys do, we explored the back roads and byways of our neighbourhood, and often people would dump the garbage and whatever they were cleaning out of the house. From time to time we'd come across pornographic books of a harder nature, more graphic you might say, [of] a more explicit nature than we would encounter, let's say, in your local grocery store . . . The most damaging kinds of pornography are those that involve violence and sexual violence. Because the wedding of these two forces, as I know only too well, brings about behaviour that is just too terrible to describe.

'. . . (It's) like an addiction, you keep craving something harder, harder. Something which gives you a greater sense of excitement. Until you reach the point where the pornography only goes so far. You reach that jumping-off point where you begin to wonder if maybe actually doing it will give you that which is beyond just reading about it or looking at it.[7]

Sex is often seen, by men in particular, as a way to attain real power, to dominate and subdue someone else, bringing them into line with your will. Richard J. Foster urges us to understand that: 'We cannot look at the crimes of incest and rape, without realising that these are crimes of power. Sex is power, real power.

There is nothing neutral or passive about it. It is alive with spiritual energy.'[8]

Pornographic material has the power to fill our thought life with fantasy, dangerous fantasy. Dangerous, because this fantasy allows us to use other people for our own ends, without respect for their thoughts or feelings. We can imagine all sorts of things which involve someone else only as an entity, a thing to be manipulated to serve our own ends.

Cummings, Goddard and Smith have expressed this well in their book, *Twentieth Century Sex*. 'If fantasies are uncontrolled, they spiral further and further from reality. Other people feature in them simply as stereotypes, one dimensional images conjured up for pleasure —not real human beings with needs and feelings of their own.

'. . . fantasy is only ever an appetiser. It sharpens our senses and gets us ready for the real thing; but on its own it's incapable of delivering satisfaction. It feeds on our energies with hypnotic appeal; a constant supply of new images is required in order to keep the pleasure coming. It gives us illusions of power and dominance as we fantasise about some ideal sexual partner offering us all we ever wanted.'[9]

Unfortunately, the end result of feeding off fantasy is an even more lonely and powerless life, as old inadequacies eventually reassert themselves. Even more tragic is the effect one person's addiction to fantasy can have on innocent bystanders. This is Bundy's legacy. If pornography has made fantasy a business, it is a business of destruction, heartache and sometimes violence.

3
Get Me Out Of Here!

Substance Use And Abuse

It was the decade of alternative lifestyles, free love, peace demonstrations and flower power. It was also the decade for acid trips and psychedelia. It was the '60s. It meant experimentation; the dawning of a new age, the age of Aquarius. To this generation came a self-styled prophet, one Timothy Leary, the LSD guru. He told everyone to 'tune in, turn on (to drugs) and drop out,' and millions did.

Today, illicit drugs are big business. In the USA, the third most valuable cash crop each year is marijuana—it brings in a cool £4.3 billion per annum. Some authorities say that by the time the present teenage generation reaches the age of 25, one out of every five will have tried either hallucinogens, stimulants, cocaine or sedatives.

In Australia, one in every three deaths among those aged 15 to 34 years is drug-related. In this age group, opiates account for 14% of all drug-related deaths.[1]

In many parts of our teenage subculture, drug overdose seems to be the most popular method of attempted suicide. Although only a small percentage of suicides among the young involves drug overdose, many more young people try to overdose than the suicide figures show.

Young people who decide to take this route often find that obtaining the actual drugs is not difficult at all. We live in a society where many people resort to swallowing things to make themselves feel better. It is not difficult for teenagers to obtain drugs from their parents' supplies or to go to a doctor, complain of sleeplessness, and have medication prescribed. Often doctors are too busy, and sometimes too complacent, to investigate a young person's complaint more fully. A few minutes in a surgery will not open the lines of communication needed. The most popular drug used in youth suicides in this country is the pill prescribed for depression.

For society, the loss of lives represents the most drastic but not the only consequence of drug abuse. A former deputy commissioner of the Victoria Police makes this comment: 'Drugs like heroin, amphetamines, hashish and cocaine, not only produce numerous users, but bring about: organised crime, a large amount of general crime, high level corruption, gang rivalry and assassination, prostitution, serious health problems, congestion of the judicial and penal systems, and large expenditure of government revenue.'[2]

Family conflict and breakdown can be added to this list.

Going Up?

Two types of drugs often associated with depressed young people are amphetamines and barbiturates—known colloquially, because of their effects, as 'uppers' and 'downers' respectively.

Amphetamines are medical drugs which are prescribed for a range of conditions, but they are often abused. Initially they make the user feel alert and full of energy. Tiredness is kept at bay and many students, wanting to study for long periods, use them to stretch their waking hours. While the user feels his thinking has sharpened, he may actually be speaking or writing total gibberish. The effects last for up to four hours and, as the user becomes habituated to amphetamine, larger doses are needed to produce the required effect.

At high levels, amphetamine causes so much stimulation that the user becomes restless, irritable and unable to sleep. Hence the drug's nickname, 'speed'. Appetite is depressed and delirium and hallucinations can appear. When the body can no longer cope with this level of constant stimulation the user experiences the amphetamine 'crash', marked by heavy and unsatisfying sleep. It takes several days for the after affects to wear off.

Amphetamine is said not to be physically addictive, but heavy users are definitely hooked psychologically, feeling unable to cope without the stimulation. Amphetamine psychosis (a condition not unlike schizophrenia) can develop, making the user depressed and sometimes suicidal—often, long after they've given up the drug.

Because 'speed' is not difficult to manufacture, large amounts are now being produced illegally. A poor quality substance often results and it may be 'cut' (adulterated) with other dangerous materials.

Barbiturates have the opposite effect. They are powerful sedatives mainly used as sleeping pills. The risk of addiction with these is also high. Initially, they produce effects similar to alcohol, making the user feel relaxed and happy. As the dose is increased, the sedative effects cause drowsiness and the user becomes clumsy and aggressive—or simply unconscious. Overdosage is not uncommon and can cause death, by interfering with breathing.

'Downers' are strongly addictive—some experts say more addictive than heroin—and withdrawal brings on irritability, insomnia and sometimes fits. Long-term use can cause physical illness, such as pneumonia, or brain damage. They are particularly dangerous when taken with alcohol.

The Party Drug

Cocaine has been labelled the 'social' or 'party' drug because of the rapid and overwhelming 'high' or 'rush' it produces which lasts for 15 to 20 minutes. Between 21 and 24 million people are believed to have tried the drug in the USA alone.

Cocaine is a white powder produced from the Central and South American cocoa plant. In the time of the Sherlock Holmes stories it was usually injected into the body but nowadays most cocaine is taken by sniffing the powder up a rolled paper tube or, in more affluent circles, using a special, gold tube worn as a piece of jewellery around the neck.

It has been reported that half of all users risk addiction and, because of its very high price, cocaine is usually 'cut' with glucose or even amphetamine.

Cocaine is a powerful stimulant causing euphoria, feelings of mental stimulation and increased physical strength. Heavy usage can produce violent and agitated behaviour, and occasionally hallucinations or even death through respiratory or heart failure.

With long-term use, any pleasant effects diminish and are often replaced altogether by nervousness, irrational fears and difficulty in sleeping. Delusions of persecution can set in, along with horrible sensations such as feelings of insects crawling on the skin. Years of 'sniffing' can also eat away at the lining of the nose causing irreparable damage.

Pot

It has been claimed in the past that marijuana smoking presents lesser risks than tobacco smoking. One study conducted by the University of California has put that theory to rest. It found that one marijuana cigarette is as bad for the body as four or five tobacco cigarettes, and regular 'pot' users may face the same lung cancer risk as pack-a-day smokers. One marijuana 'joint' deposits four times as much tar in the lungs as one tobacco cigarette, and results in five times as much carbon monoxide in the bloodstream.[3]

Marijuana is simply the dried and chopped leaves of the cannabis or hemp plant. It is smoked, often mixed with tobacco. Marijuana is a depressant drug, with initial effects similar to those induced by alcohol: relaxation, talkativeness and general animation or happiness. However, like alcohol, its depressant substance and sedative effects slow the user down and affect coordination. Larger or continued doses may cause a distorted sense of time and, occasionally, panic.

So what connection might marijuana have with depression in young people? As with all addictive drugs, long-term users gradually need larger and larger doses of marijuana to produce the same 'high'. Chronic users, who are continuously intoxicated with this drug often become apathetic and withdrawn. But the real danger is with those people who have existing or potential psychiatric problems. Like other drugs, marijuana can spark off short-lived emotional disorders, and therefore contribute to periods of depression and emotional instability.

The World's Worst

It is recognised as the world's most serious drug problem. It is heroin abuse. First developed in 1898 as a drug to treat the problem of morphine addiction, heroin—technically known as diamorphine—has become a modern killer. 'Pure' heroin, supplied as a white powder or in small stony pellets, is many times more potent and addictive than morphine.

Heroin normally finds its way into the human body via injections made directly into veins or under the skin. It is also sniffed as powder or as fumes from melted heroin, and is sometimes swallowed.

Heroin and related substances like pethidine are the most potent painkillers known. They work by slowing down the activity of the nervous system and producing a euphoria which seems to make the pain less relevant to the sufferer. They do not actually remove the pain itself. This is why heroin is so liable to abuse. Heroin produces an instant high when taken occasionally, followed by a steady calm and relaxed state which can last for several hours.

Even at low doses, however, it slows the movement of food through the digestive system, causing constipation. In larger doses it becomes attached to the nervous system and begins to change the way nerve impulses travel through the brain. Addiction becomes a vicious cycle— progressively larger doses of the drug are needed to achieve the same level of euphoria, as the body develops tolerance of these effects. At higher doses long-term effects develop. Among these are chronic constipation, loss of interest in food and sex, and interference with the menstrual cycle. The drug begins to dominate every area of life.

Withdrawal from heroin addiction is a frightening experience for most heavy users as it involves more than physical effects. Withdrawal brings on psychological feelings of tremendous vulnerability and loneliness. It is a very solitary state of mind. Heavy users continue taking the drug long after the early euphoric experiences have ceased, simply to avoid the crushing feelings of withdrawal. During withdrawal, users yearn for a 'fix' to numb their senses.

Another tragic issue associated with heroin abuse is that, because of its high price as an illicit drug, it is usually adulterated with other substances before being sold to the user. Sometimes inert substances such as glucose, milk and sugar are mixed in, causing few additional problems. But all sorts of contaminants may be used—including talcum powder, flour, brick dust and even scouring powder. When injected straight into the bloodstream these can have serious effects—potentially worse than the heroin itself!

Heroin can also cause death as a result of impaired breathing. This substance contributes directly to the general downhill slide which so many young lives are taking. It is a slide which often ends in death, either through the addiction itself, or by suicide brought on by associated severe depression and despair.

The Booze Bandit.

'Yesterday, the mother of a 14-year-old boy who was electrocuted when he climbed on top of a moving train, said he had a drinking problem . . . She said she had intended to send him to Alcoholics Anonymous.'

I read these words in a leading newspaper and felt my

stomach turn. Alcoholics Anonymous already has a special section for dealing with 17- to 25-year-old booze addicts. But now we have a growing number of 11 and 12 year-olds being hauled up before childrens' courts across the land, on drink-related charges. The booze bandit is having a field day with our young people.

In some parts of Australia, up to 87% of children aged 12 to 16 years drink. Seventy-five percent of all drug-related-deaths in the 15 to 34 year age group are due to alchohol.[4] It is the most significant cause of death for people in that age group, bringing many lives to a sudden end in horrific road accidents. It's time we declared war on this merciless addiction.

Alcohol is a poison!

Alcohol is absorbed very rapidly into the blood stream and is carried to the brain. It is often known to produce at first feelings of exhilaration and confidence, relaxing inhibitions. But it is actually a depressant substance. Often, once the initial high is gone, after a number of drinks, lack of co-ordination, slurred speech and all the classic symptoms of drunkenness set in. Of course, the amount of alcohol needed to produce these affects varies from person to person.

Most people don't understand, or won't admit to, what makes an alcoholic. Many alcoholics do not sleep on park benches by night, or walk the streets by day looking for food. This is the popular view of an alcoholic. In fact, most alcoholics seldom appear drunk. Most are people who show no outward sign of being addicted. An alcoholic is someone who cannot function without alcohol and, tragically, many alcoholics are young!

For alcoholics, withdrawal can mean going through

delirium tremors (DT's), which involve frightening hallucinations. They live in bondage to a body, soul and brain-destroying chemical. So many of our teenagers are prepared to risk that without ever stopping to consider just why people start drinking in the first place.

Some young people get into alcohol because they think it will gain them acceptance with their peers. Peer group pressure is all about people, who don't feel good about themselves, trying to build their self-esteem. They do so by reducing everyone else to their lowest common denominator. So many young people are trying desperately to be average—just so that everyone will be comfortable having them around. What a rip-off!

Some young people start drinking because they think it makes them appear mature, even sophisticated. But people are at their most unsophisticated when they've 'had a few'. What's so mature about forgetting how to walk?

For others, alcohol is the way to numb the senses and kill the pain of hurt emotions and broken relationships. Alcohol is worn like a mask. It gives 'dutch' courage to the fearful and insecure. But it is only a mask! Alcohol can't help a person solve their problems, it can't help an individual overcome guilt, anger or inferiority. It simply covers them up temporarily.

Many people never learn to control their drinking and each year statistics are published which ought to sober up any regular drinker. Each year over 3000 die of alcohol-related causes. Alcohol accounts for between 20% and 30% of all hospital admissions and is involved in 66% of all murders. Its influence can be found in 40% of all serious road accidents, 30% of drownings and 20% of all suicides.[5] Yet alcohol is painted in the media, and throughout society generally, as being an important part of social interaction without any mention being made of these possible consequences of its abuse.

In one year, 1,500 young adults (aged between 15 and 34 years) died as a direct result of drug abuse. Over 1,000 of them owed their untimely death to alcohol abuse.[6] When you add to this the 140 children aged 14 years or under who were killed in drink-related road accidents that year, you begin to see the size of our alcohol problem as it relates to youth.

The powerful emotional and psychological effects of alcohol also appear in studies of other youth-related social problems. Several studies have shown that adolescents who start to drink at an early age are more likely to engage in deviant behaviour—such as driving a car without a licence, damaging property, stealing and running away from home.

Smoking Is A Life Hazard

It might seem strange to include here a section on tobacco smoking. After all, who would seriously contemplate suicide by cigarette? The fact is, while cigarette smoking will not usually kill a person immediately, it very often contributes to a slower process of death. In 1977, the Royal College of Physicians published a statement saying that a smoker's lifespan is shortened by about five and a half minutes for every cigarette he or she smokes. It doesn't take mathematical genius to deduce the long-term implications of this. If a smoker lights up just five cigarettes per day, 35 per week—some people smoke more than that every day—his or her life would be shortened by three hours each week, 13 hours per month and seven days every year.

Drug death studies undertaken in this country reveal time and again that tobacco smoking is, by a large margin, the biggest killer of Australians of all ages. In 1985, 81% of drug-related deaths in this country, over all age-groups, were due to tobacco use. Over 17,000 people died of tobacco-related causes. Now, it must be said that, in that year, no-one under the age of 34 died as a result of tobacco use. But the figures are alarming for those aged over 35.[7]

The point is, we ought to be concerning ourselves not just with the present well-being of our young people, but with their long-term health and happiness. Smoking tobacco may not be a way to kill yourself suddenly, but it still kills. And of all the drugs we have discussed, it is often thought by teenagers to be the least dangerous.

Many teenagers do not even think of tobacco as a drug. They remain unaware that, as with heroin, nicotine produces true physiological addiction, with direct affects on the mind and body. As with other addictive drugs, the body quickly develops tolerance to tobacco. Progressively higher doses are then needed to produce the same effects.

Nicotine is a powerful stimulant. When inhaled in tobacco smoke it increases pulse rate and blood pressure, reducing skin temperature and appetite. Some world authorities have claimed that, if all smoking were to cease, we would cut out 90% of all lung and throat cancer cases, 33% of heart disease cases, 50% of bladder cancer deaths and 85% of bronchitis and emphysema deaths. That's a lot of cutting back.

We need to encourage our young people to leave this often overlooked drug menace alone.

Why Drugs?

It is sometimes hard for people who have never really been introduced to today's drug culture, to understand exactly what motivates a young person to become involved with drugs of dependency. I think, without oversimplifying what can be a very complex issue, we can identify three basic reasons for a teenager's excursion into drug experiences.

I have already touched briefly on the aspect of peer group pressure. Some adolescents begin experimenting with drugs because of a desire to belong to a group. Alcohol is now more of a status symbol than popping pills or smoking dope. It has a tougher image associated with it. Many young adolescents are looking for an aggressive image. Alcohol helps them achieve that. We all fear being unloved. Many young people are devaluing themselves in various ways for cheap acceptance.

Take, for example, the young girl who submits to pressure from her boyfriend to sleep with him. She does so, knowing that, as many surveys have indicated, the great majority of young single men would prefer to marry a virgin. Cheap acceptance!

Think too of all the young men out there who, because of peer expectations, hide behind a mask of nonchalance, bravado and 'machoism'. They are afraid to openly express their true feelings. They suppress vulnerability, hiding hurts and traumas that grow to become like time bombs of anger within them. It is possible that some of our domestic violence, and the street shootings of recent years, might have been avoided if men had felt comfortable about venting pent-up emotions at an earlier age. When young men turn to drugs, it is often a sign that they are deeply traumatised, lonely and alienated.

An important concept here is that of the 'reference group'. A reference group is a collection of persons who served as a point of influence concerning a particular attitude or behaviour. For most teenagers, reference groups will include people such as rock musicians, school leaders, athletes, TV or movie idols. All may have an influence on the adolescent's views on drug-taking.

Another important reference group is the family. Data collected in studies all over the world indicates that, when asked why they first drank alcohol, most teenagers say that peer group pressure had much to do with it. A large percentage indicate that they drank for the first time at home or at a family celebration. This suggests that parents do have some control over whether their child is likely to start drinking.

Before we castigate the young over their problems with drugs, we need to recognise that parents sometimes contribute to them. Popping pills to cope with life's difficulties is becoming a way of life for so many adults in our community. The young are usually less equipped to exercise restraint with potentially dangerous drugs. But too often parents lecture their children on drugs with a 'don't do as I do, do as I say' mentality. (More on that in part two of this book).

Some parents even encourage their teenagers to experiment with drugs. There are fathers who pat their sons on the back when they come home drunk. After all, they think, it's better for their sons to drink, than to be into 'real' drugs! Yet alcohol is as real and as potentially dangerous a drug as any other.

Aside from the influence of peer or reference groups, one of the most important reasons teenagers turn to drugs is their inability to deal with problems. When young people feel they cannot cope with the pressures of life, they may look for ways to escape or numb their senses.

In families which experience severe problems, such as child abuse, or emotional disturbance, taking drugs can be part of a teenager's coping mechanism. The story of Russ Campbell illustrates this. In this case, his drug dependency reappeared in later life, with tragic consequences.

Russ tried to time his suicide for his 34th birthday. He missed by a few hours. As a boy he had found it diffficult to live with a war veteran alcoholic as a father. At 14 years of age he was drinking and soon became involved with car thefts and minor burglaries. He was sent to a boys' corrective institution and seemed set for a life of crime when, suddenly, he joined Alcoholic Anonymous. It changed his life.

He began to work with other troubled young people in crisis-help centres and for over 10 years he was, in his mother's words, 'a tower of strength.' He married and had t.vo lovely children. He watched them grow and was a happy family man for those 10 years. Sadly, though, his life then took another turn for the worse. He was involved in a car accident and his marriage broke up, his children leaving to live with their mother. Here I let his mother complete the story:

'Maybe it was the drugs Russ was given to help with his injuries, maybe the grief at the loss of his children. But he seemed intent on destroying himself. He resumed drinking and took any drug.

'Then one night . . . I found him smashing his head against a cement path in the garden . . . Russ said he couldn't possibly beat drugs again. He had made his way up once, but he was tired. 'He said to me: "The kindest thing I can give you for my birthday is my death!" If they cremate me six times, I will never forget the sound of his head hitting the concrete.'[8]

Russ Campbell died of a drug overdose at 11 pm on May 3, 1988. How many other Russ Campbells are out there—how many children who are even now developing self-defeating patterns of behaviour to help them cope with anger, fear or bitterness?

A third factor in a teenager's involvement with drugs, may be that young people seem to possess an in-built mechanism for taking risks. Why do young people spend mega-dollars going to see movies which cannot be classified as works of art? Movies which are thin in the plot department, weak in the acting department, but packed with action. Basically, because they relate to heroic, larger-than-life characters and stories. Teenagers want to identify with someone who is leading a more exciting life than they are. Why do some teens plaster pop-posters all over their bedroom walls, ensuring that the rockers of this world get pride of place in the decor? Because young people like to look up and dream about living glamorous lives in the fast lane, in the circles those idols mix in.

Risk-taking behaviour is a part of this 'adventure drive'. Pushing the limits of safe behaviour gets the adrenalin pumping. Experimentation can be fun. Sadly, young people who have not had the benefit of a secure home life, or been taught a healthy self-respect, often take the wrong kinds of risk. Experimentation with drugs can begin as a game, a display of curiosity which eventually leads to sickness and even death. We should never underestimate the power of human curiosity—particularly in the young.

Drugs and Despair
It's no coincidence that most youth suicide attempts happen under the influence of alcohol or some other

drug. As one magazine writer put it: 'A problem that could seem difficult when you're 'straight', can seem totally impossible when you're 'out of it'.' Drugs do not help make solutions clearer. Their influence can confuse the issue even more. At best, they can provide temporary relief from traumatised feelings—relief that will cost the user in other areas. At worst, they can add significantly to the physiological and emotional symptoms of depression.

There is a good deal of despair in our society when it comes to the whole drug issue. Some say there is much to despair about. A 1987 report published by the Commonwealth Department of Health in Australia found that, assuming people have a normal life expectancy of 70 years, an estimated 233,000 years of life were lost in 1985 through drug abuse. That's a lot of life for a small nation to lose.

Added to the direct effects of drug-taking on people in the community, are the problems associated with shared syringes and the AIDS virus. The despair surrounding this issue came home to me when I picked up an AIDS awareness leaflet, published by the Health Department of Victoria. One clearly marked paragraph told people what number to call if they wanted to know more about needles and syringes. Here's some of the advice given:

'Sharing needles and syringes is the easiest way to get infected with the AIDS virus. If you use drugs in this way ALWAYS USE YOUR OWN NEEDLE AND SYRINGE. If you can't get one BOIL the one you've got or soak it in bleach ... first and use afterwards' (Capitals are theirs).[9]

There is a degree of hopeless resignation in a statement like that. I'm not advocating against the use of pamphlets to make kids aware of the dangers they face, but I do object to the fact that we make certain ills, like drug addiction, seem incurable. It sounds as if the writers of this pamphlet—a state government body—are telling our youth: 'We can't help you with your heroin problem—you'll probably die with that in a few years anyway—but perhaps we can at least stop you catching AIDS.'

Despair is not what is needed here. We need to see the drug problem as not just a cause of youth traumas, but a symptom of them. If we are ever to ease the teenage drug problem we must deal with underlying problems such as the disintegration of the home, alienation from parents and parental support, and confusion regarding workable value systems.

We can make changes, if we get the foundations right.

Jesus Christ said it so well: If you build on rock, on right priorities and godly values, founded upon moral absolutes, you will stand up to the pressure tests of life; if you build your life and the lives of your children on sand, on shifting humanistic and materialistic values, you can expect a traumatic time when the rains fall.

We need, now more than ever, to teach teenagers absolutes, to give them realistic, but noble standards to live up to. We need to look again at the Bible and allow its ancient but eternal wisdom to speak to our lives. Without faith in God this drug burdened generation may have every reason to despair. But I have personally shared with and counselled so many young people whose drug-affected lives have been turned around through a close encounter of the very best kind—a personal revelation of Jesus Christ.

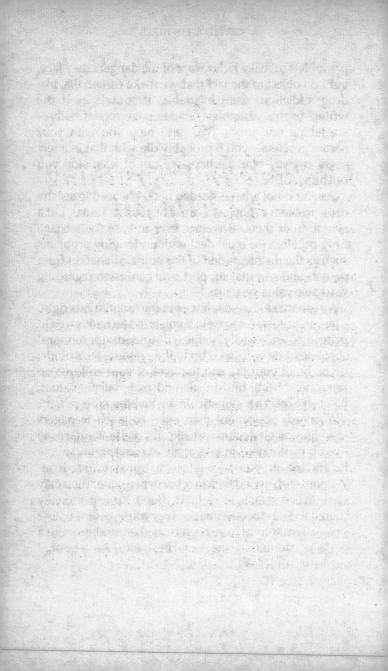

4

I Believe In Everything – A Little Bit

Moral Confusion

'Make love not war . . . peace, brother! . . . free love . . . liberation!' These were the catchcries of the younger generation during the heady and turbulent 1960s. Youthful lives were charged with idealism. Many young people shared a commitment to ridding the world of war and destruction and ushering in a new age of peaceful coexistence.

As they rebelled against an establishment that fell short of their ideals, many young people partly abandoned traditional morality. They favoured life under the banner of sexual liberation. Unfortunately though, a new generation now deals with the despair and bewilderment of the '90s. If the '60s were liberated, the '80s are confused! Social researcher Richard Eckersley says: 'Australia has become more pluralistic and hetrogeneous . . . While young people may no longer be under the same pressure to conform [as they were prior to the 60's] . . . they now face a bewildering array of values and beliefs to choose from.'[1]

The casting-off of traditional morals, has left adolescents today with little framework for life and choice. Situation ethic, for all its good intentions, has forced teenagers to confront issues their parents did not face at the same age.

As historian Manning Clarke has put it: 'We live in an age of doubt about everything.' Kids are expected to make choices for which neither life experience nor parental influence have prepared them.

Much of what adult liberals call progressive in our 'new morality' contains absurd contradictions. Society tells the young that aborting unborn human beings is perfectly reasonable, but forest trees, whales and dolphins must be saved at all costs. Can anyone seriously blame young people for feeling just a little confused? Perhaps they are prepared to be more honest about the absurdities of our moral systems.

The Heat Is On

More young people are experiencing emotional burn-out from sexual promiscuity than from perhaps any other quarter.

It is a biological fact that puberty is 'arriving' earlier today than in previous generations. One hundred years ago, the average age for the onset of puberty was around 16 years. Forty years ago, that age had dropped to 14 years. Today, it stands at 12 years, and is decreasing. This, according to youth writer Josh McDowell, means that: 'Great physical changes and their attendant feelings hit when kids are younger and less mature emotionally than has been the case in the past. It also means that, even if young people today were to marry at the same ages as in the past, they still have several more years during which they have to keep their feelings and desires under control.'[2]

This comes at a time when sexual fantasy is being sold to teenagers as never before. The money-makers of the movies, music and advertising industries peddle sex in a way that would have been unthinkable a few years ago. Music has been like a second language for teenagers since the 1950s. In the unashamedly materialistic post-World War Two era, teenagers were suddenly blessed with disposable incomes of their own, and marketers quickly invented new and exciting ways for them to spend. Music held an obvious attraction for the young —especially when it contained elements of rebellion and self-indulgence. Before long a new culture within a culture was born. Kids now spoke a language their parents couldn't understand, listened to music their parents found cacophonous, and wore clothes their parents 'would not be seen dead in'. All this was worn as a badge of defiant independence.

Rock'n'roll and pop music provided a new kind of sex education for a daring new breed. Sex has featured heavily in song lyrics from the early days of the youth music industry. At one time 'sex, drugs and rock'n'roll' were seen as essential parts of truly liberated life. Today, drugs have fallen out of favour with some kids, but sex and music are closer partners than ever before.

In the past two decades lyrics have become more explicit and references to sex far less cloaked in ambiguity. A song from Salt'N'Pepa is entitled *Push It*, which leaves little to the imagination in itself. The lyrics, the few there are, speak of feverish love-making and sexual orgasm. One line says: 'Can't you hear the music pumping, like I wish you would?'

Just as blatant is George Michael's *I Want Your Sex*. He tells us it's simply a song about responsible relationships, yet it openly describes a young man's attempts to get his girlfriend drunk so that he can keep her in his room and sleep with her.

A song about responsibility? Really? In an age where thousands are dying of AIDS and other sexually transmitted diseases are rampant, Michael, a leading light in the pop-rock industry, gives a portrayal of sex which demeans the people involved. This kind of devaluing influence pervades much of the music regularly aimed at the teenage market.

On the small screen video-clip market, according to the Australian writer and speaker John Smith, stars such as Madonna and Cher are 'selling themselves like whores.' In their case this is seen as being acceptable, he says, because 'they make big bucks.'[3] Such role models do little to help kids develop a healthy respect for sexuality.

Earlier puberty is expanding adolescence downward, but social pressures are causing many young people to marry later. Fifty years ago, marriage usually signalled the beginning of a young person's sexual experience and, generally speaking, young people then married earlier in life than they do now. Even if the proportion of youth keeping their virginity until marriage was the same today as it was half a century ago, and they were marrying at the same age as they were then, they would still have to control their sexual drives for longer. Today, often more than 12 years pass between the onset of puberty and the time a person marries. In that time, many adolescents deal with their strong hormonal drives through brief sexual encounters which do not satisfy their deep needs for affection and commitment.

Also, while young people are being taught the actual mechanics of sex earlier than previous generations, they may not be better equipped for it emotionally. Josh

McDowell cites two reasons for this.[4] Young people today have, he says, less contact with adults in their families than did their forebears. The breakdown in the extended family has left many teenagers without the wide range of adult interactions which was available to kids in years gone by. These days, a teenager's grandfathers, grandmothers, aunts and uncles often live many miles from him or her, whereas in previous generations they may have lived within walking distance.

Parents too have less interaction with their children today. One feature of an ever-increasing number of marriages is that both partners are holding down fulltime jobs. They leave in their wake a generation of 'latchkey kids' who basically take care of themselves in after school hours. The opportunities for meaningful interaction between teenagers and their parents are thus diminished. Fifty years ago, the average child had three to four hours of interaction each day with parents or extended family members. Today the average child has only about 15 minutes of this much needed interaction,[5] and much of this time is spent with parents laying down or reinforcing rules, or criticising.

Secondly, McDowell cites the instability and insecurity of family relationships as a major factor in teenage sexual problems. Family breakdowns happen so frequently and affect so many people in teenage peer groups, that many kids have little reason to believe in the viability of the family unit. When young people are also the victims of child sexual abuse, they may have every reason to feel cynical about relationships in general.

The consequences of increased teenage sexual activity are obvious. The most obvious result is teen pregnancy. In the US, where more figures are available on this, more than one million teenage girls become pregnant each year and 80% are unmarried. Of those teenage girls who do marry, 60% will be divorced within five years and 60% of them will be pregnant again within two years.[6] Unwanted pregnancies have made life very difficult for thousands of our young girls.

Sexually transmitted diseases are also a greater problem today than a generation ago. They are more widespread and, because people are becoming sexually active at an earlier age, more teenagers face the risk of infection than ever before. We shall look at this subject shortly.

Perhaps less obvious than the physical effects of such diseases, but just as real, are the emotional and psychological scars which are so often a legacy of adolescent pre-marital sex. Unfulfilling relationships frequently leave young people with a tremendous sense of disillusionment regarding sex and relationships. Many become suspicious of marriage. Feelings of guilt and low self-esteem set in when a young person feels he or she has been used. Some also wonder whether a future spouse will appreciate knowing they've been sexually active before. Some homosexuals and lesbians have testified that their disillusionment with heterosexual relationships began as a result of unpleasant or unrewarding early sexual encounters.

All you need is lust ...

Said one wise and observant man: 'The only thing we learn from history is that we never learn from history.' As James Dobson observes: 'Mankind has known intuitively for at least fifty centuries that indiscriminate sexual activity represents both an individual and a corporate threat to survival.'[7]

In conducting an exhaustive study of 88 civilisations

which have existed at different times in the earth's history, anthropologist J.D. Unwin noted that each had exhibited a similar life cycle. Each began with a fairly strict moral code and ended with the call for 'freedom' to express individual passions. There were no exceptions to this rule.[8]

Sexual permissiveness has been the rot eating away at the foundations of civilisations for millenia. There is a clear link between the growth and survival of a culture and its attitude to sexual morality. Why is this? 'It is because the energy that holds people together is sexual in nature!' writes Dobson. 'The physical attraction between men and women causes them to establish a family and invest themselves in its development. It encourages them to work and save and toil to insure the survival of their families. Their sexual energy provides the impetus for the raising of healthy children and for the transfer of values from one generation to another ... in short, the sexual aspect of our nature—when released exclusively within the family—produces stability and responsibility that would not otherwise occur. When a nation is composed of millions of devoted, responsible family units, the entire society is stable, responsible and resilient.'[9]

The Great Love Myths

History demonstrates the need for properly disciplined sexuality, yet today's youth are being subjected to some potent misinformation about what love actually is. Modern teenagers are asked to believe three major myths regarding love relationships. The first is that to be independent is to be truly free: To have no strings attached, and to be answerable to no-one, is what freedom is all about.

Remember the Marlboro man? He used to sit high in the saddle, puffing on a piece of Marlboro weed, completely at peace with himself—alone and in control of his destiny. He could come and go as he pleased, there were no cumbersome restrictions on his freedom. He owed nothing to anybody. There were no commitments, no responsibilities except to himself. He was a man's man. The life of the Marlboro man is a great one—except, of course, if you happen to be Mrs. Marlboro man, or one of the Marlboro kids! You see, he doesn't know a thing about commitment and commitment is what relationships are all about.

Marilyn Monroe was once asked about her beliefs. She said 'I just believe in everything, a little bit.' That's called keeping your options open! Some kids today will only ever make one commitment in life—the commitment to keeping their options open. Sex is most rewarding when it is based on commitment and trust.

The second of today's great love myths is that sex and intimacy are one and the same thing. Unfortunately, millions of broken hearts the world over will agree that you can be sexually involved with someone without ever really knowing them. You might sleep with a person with whom you've never been able to share your deepest thoughts, fears or aspirations. As one young man put it: 'It's easier today to bare your bottom, than to bare your soul.'

This at a time in history when intimacy is at a premium. McDowell writes that 'what we've had over the past twenty years is not so much a sexual revolution as a revolution in the search for intimacy. Human beings desperately need intimacy. In the past, that need was met before marriage in families by one's parents and siblings. With the breakup and insecurity in modern families, however, many young people turn to sexual relationships in the vain hope that they will provide the needed intimacy.'[10]

Were you ever taught as a kid, as I was, that you only value things when they've cost you something? Sex without intimacy comes too cheaply and is less highly valued, and less rewarding, as a result. Millions of young people are not being taught that it is possible to confuse emotion for devotion. No wonder we are finding that couples wake up one morning to find that the flame of their love for each other has flickered and gone out, seemingly overnight. The relationship busts up, usually not without bitterness. Why? Often it's because the parties have not built intimacy into their relationship. They settled for emotional or physical 'highs' alone.

The third of the great sex lies foisted upon teenagers is that today is all there is. According to this philosophy, the highest good we can do is to live for the now—to forget about the future and just have a good time. Randy Stonehill, the Christian singer and comic, sums this one up so well when he sings, ' . . . So have a good time . . . and die young.' There is an urgency about the way some kids live today. They want to cram a lifetime of experience into a few short youthful years. Little wonder so many are burning out before their time!

As a society we have largely lost our sense of accountability, not just to each other, but to God. Once human beings were acutely aware of their dependence on the Creator, or at least some higher power. The weather that determined the success of the harvest, and therefore our economic survival, was in His hands, as was physical health. In societies which embrace Christian ethics, people believed that one day they would be held accountable by God for the way in which they used

His resources. People were stewards of God's gifts, caretakers of His world, and responsible ultimately to Him. Death was not the end of existence. It was the doorway to reward or punishment, depending on how we had handled life in the body.

The Pilgrim Fathers stepped off a ship onto American soil and immediately held a thanksgiving service to show their gratitude to the Almighty for getting them there in one piece. It's hard to imagine the modern business executive stepping out of the Boeing jet and kissing the tarmac in worship of God! It seems we just don't seem to need God the way we once did. His benefits are long forgotten, now attributed to the 'wonders of modern science.' For centuries, however, developing civilisations were held morally on track by the idea that man must answer to his Maker. By conveniently forgetting the idea of coming judgement, we have lost our sense of accountability as a society and have compromised our moral strength.

Bruce Wilson observes that we have become adept at using 'social science jargon which makes us think of our behaviour merely in terms of neurological necessity, psychological destiny and sociological fate ... as if we are not moral agents responsible for the way we respond to our fate at all. We are beginning to excuse not only our own sins in the name of psychiatry or sociology, but also the sins of assassins, murderers, rapists and child molesters.'[11]

What does this have to do with youth sexuality? The answer is plain: sex without accountability is sex devoid of commitment. Abandoning God has been just the first step in watering down the whole concept of being answerable to others for what we do. We want to do our own thing without asking permission or needing to submit our will to the will of another. Sex has only suffered under this kind of regime. So often, marriage has failed because it has been seen as little more than legalised lust and couples have split up without ever experiencing the joys of unselfish commitment. Put simply, many have failed to think ahead about where their present actions will take them in the long term.

We need to be teaching our young people the need for commitment in relationships. This can only come as we bow to the idea of accountability in other areas of life too. We need to encourage the youth of our society to think ahead about the consequences of their present actions. 'You reap what you sow' needs to become a modern axiom.

'You shall be like gods'

Our society seems to want the freedom to make choices without suffering the consequences of bad choices. We want to have our cake and eat it. This is clear in society's attitude to abortion.

An unwanted pregnancy presents massive problems for an adolescent girl. She may face the wrath or unsupportiveness of her parents and she may find that she is far from emotionally prepared for motherhood. The pregnancy may present financial problems, if she is without caring support from family and friends. Having a baby might very well mean that all of her plans for the future, for a career and so on, need to be changed, postponed, or shelved for good. Her whole life may be thrown into turmoil.

The Family Planning Association based in Richmond, Victoria, conducted a survey of over 2,000 first-time attenders at its clinic. The survey showed that more than half of these women had not used contraceptives at their first experience of intercourse. The median age of those who responded was 21 years and only 13% were married. The average age for first intercourse was $17^1/_2$ years.[12]

Of those aged under 15 years at their first attendance at the clinic, only about 16% had used contraception during their first intercourse.[13] If these women can be taken to represent the wider population, we see that the great majority of young women stand a good chance of becoming pregnant after their very first experience with sex. Perhaps even more sad is the fact that of those surveyed, only 4% described their first act of intercourse as 'fantastic'. Almost two-thirds described it as 'no big deal', 'uncomfortable' or 'disastrous'. Just teaching teenagers the physical mechanics of sex does not prepare them for emotional involvement.

The saddest finding of this study was the fact that more than half the women surveyed had abortions when they became pregnant. In this country 100,000 abortions are performed each year. Among these are many cases of multiple abortions. Over one quarter of all the abortions performed in Australia each year are carried out on teenage girls.[14]

One newspaper decided to look into the sensitive area of teenage abortion and published the story of 'Zoe'. The report was headed: 'Zoe, 16, decides school is more vital than her baby.' Zoe (not her real name) came from a middle-class Sydney suburb. She had met the young man who got her pregnant at a hotel one year before the article was written. They enjoyed a one night stand and, when she became pregnant, he had offered to pay half the bill for an abortion.

'Her parents don't know where she is today,' says the article, '[Zoe is] sitting in an abortion clinic ... She told her mother she was going out and would stay with a friend tonight . . . She is 16 and has braces on her teeth. She is ten weeks pregnant.

'Was it a hard decision to have an abortion? "Not really," she says. "It was and it wasn't. It wasn't because there was no way I wanted to leave school half way through year ten. It's a really important year." '

Reading this, I couldn't help but feel that Zoe did not really have her priorities sorted out. Is it possible that Zoe, and many others in a similar situation, might not act first and then think about the implications of their actions when it is too late? There is still a great deal of confusion and ignorance about abortion in many young minds.

Abortion: It's Not That Simple!

Some people think that abortion is the only compassionate means of helping a woman deal with an unwanted pregnancy. I don't believe that this is true. Adoption is still, in most cases, a realistic option, as is keeping the child with parental, community or church support. Even if abortion seems to the woman to be her only option, it certainly is not much of an option for the child!

From a biblical perspective, the baby is a human being right from the time he or she is conceived. A child is so much more in God's eyes than a mere bundle of cells. God is aware of the child and watches over it with the same love and concern which He feels for all people. He has a plan for the life of that child, a clear concept of what he or she could achieve in life. The baby is of inestimable value to God.

If one does not wish to look to the Bible for clues as to the status of the unborn child, one needs to look no further than Life Magazine. Lennart Nilsson has established an outstanding reputation over the years for his amazing photography of nature and, more particularly, the growth of a baby in the mother's womb. His best work to date, published in the August 1990 edition of Life, shows the development of a baby from the time conception occurs—a photo of the sperm entering the egg is stunning—up to around 11 weeks. With the aid of microscopes and cameras we can clearly see that, even after just six to eight weeks, the child is taking on the appearance of a human being.

After just 56 days the embryo, whilst only one and a half inches long, has organs which are almost all formed and in place. At six weeks, the arms and legs are short but starting to take shape. A tiny heart shows up as a red blob on the coloured photo and, although no bones have yet formed in the skull, the brain is easily seen above the eye. After seven weeks the eyes have formed and in just one more week skin begins to fold over it. By 28 weeks the eye is so sensitive to light, that if a physician peers into the uterus with a foetoscope, the foetus will try to shield its eyes with its hands.

Looking at photographs like these should be enough to convince one that abortion is not simply a matter of what is good for the mother. But just how compassionate is abortion for the mother anyway?

In some of their publications, pro-abortion lobbyists touch only briefly on negative physical side effects which can be experienced by a woman who has had an abortion. Yet complications can include: damage to the cervix, puncturing of the uterine wall and, when even the smallest piece of foetal tissue is left behind, infection and blockage in the fallopian tubes. In more serious cases, a blockage of the tubes may prevent the woman from ever having another normal pregnancy.

In the course of our research my assistant came across a pamphlet which purported to tell the whole truth about abortion. It was called *Abortion: The Facts*, and was published by a group calling themselves the Right to Choose Coalition. Here's a sample of what many young women are told about abortion: 'Most women have an abortion at some time and they certainly do not have any problem having children later.'

The tract goes on to claim that abortion is the 'most common surgical procedure in the world' and that, when conducted early in the pregnancy, it is 'ten times safer than having a baby, and fourteen times safer than having your tonsils out.' Even after 12 weeks of pregnancy, abortion, which is by now a much more risky proposition for the woman, is 'still safer for the woman than having a child.'

'Women feel tired and sometimes a bit sick for a few hours (after the abortion),' it says, 'especially if they have had a general anaesthetic. It is best if you can rest for the remainder of the day. By the next day you should be feeling well enough to go back to work or school. Some women feel a bit depressed, and have topsy-turvy emotions for a couple of weeks. This is mainly because of the change in hormones from being pregnant to being non-pregnant. Most women just feel relief to be back in charge of their lives.'[16]

For all the talk about how safe and simple abortion is, how straightforward and uncomplicated as a procedure, the fact remains that thousands of teenage girls, not to mention older women, grapple with painful feelings of guilt and grief for months and even years after an abortion. Sometimes the emotional scars are very difffficult to heal. For a young woman who already nurses such scars, the effect of other emotional traumas on her sense of self-worth can be devastating. What is perhaps most difficult for many a young woman to understand is why, when most of society says that abortion is her right, she can still feel guilty for having gone through with it.

Consider for a moment the story of Alison. Now in her early thirties, Alison relates in public meetings the agony of her experience with abortion as a young adult. Alison had begun nursing training at the time she fell pregnant. The pregnancy was unplanned—she was on the pill.

Organising to have the abortion was not difficult, even though abortion in these circumstances was illegal in the state where she lived. She simply obtained a referral from a local clinic and flew interstate for the operation. Alison left home at 11 am and was back again at 6pm the same day. The procedure itself, performed by vacuum curettage, lasted only 15 minutes. It was a straightforward medical procedure, but for Alison it was nowhere near as uncomplicated emotionally. Alison takes up her story:

'After the nurse said to me, "Go now, it's all over. The pregnancy has been destroyed," I asked whether it was a boy or a girl. They said they don't give that information. As a throw-away comment, I asked whether there was one or two. The woman replied: "There were twins." '

'I was absolutely shocked. I couldn't stop shaking. It suddenly hit me what I had done. Not one but two babies were gone—flushed away.'

Alison returned home full of remorse, having decided not to share her secret with her parents. One evening, just before she was due to leave on an overseas trip, she engaged her mother in conversation on the subject of childbirth. Alison asked her mother what she thought of abortion.

'Then Mum dropped the bombshell,' Alison recalls. 'She said she had nearly aborted me. She was the age in life when the doctor strongly recommended abortion and said I should be terminated.

'Mum turned to me and said she could never do that to a baby she was carrying. She could never believe it was right and how happy she was she had made her decision to go through with having me, despite the risk. I felt like slipping into a dark hole in the ground and never coming out.

'I had conversations with Mum and kept trying to tell her what I had done, but I couldn't get it out. I kept thinking, if only I had told her she could have talked me out of it and two children would be here today.'

A short time later, Alison came to a place of real faith in God, where she could believe that he had forgiven her. This was a great relief. Still she says: 'Today the hardest part is not forgiving myself.'[17]

Alison was fortunate enough to have a mother who positively affirmed her daughter's worth. What effect might abortion have on girls whose parents are less supportive?

Abortion is not as clear-cut as is often claimed. It can have devastating emotional and psychological effects on a young woman and, where the baby is concerned, many people in our community consider it murder. Once a pregnancy has begun, there really is no turning back. A woman, or girl, will bear that baby in her mind, even if she expels it from her body. Abortion can be soul destroying for the woman concerned. It is life destroying for the baby.

I am absolutely certain that, in their hearts, most young people know they simply cannot have their cake and eat it. They know that their moral choices have consequences. Instead of trying to create illusions about the bad decisions they can make, we should offer them greater support in making productive, positive and wise choices.

Dying In The Name Of Love.

The greatest tragedy associated with homosexuality and sexual promiscuity today is the appearance and rapid growth of the AIDS problem. Cancer is still a killer, herpes and other sexually transmitted diseases are still rife in the community but, in terms of public awareness and notoriety, all have now been eclipsed by AIDS. The problem has grown to epidemic proportions and has been called by some 'the Black Death of the twentieth century.'

Millions of people the world over have already become infected with the AIDS virus and are at risk of developing the full blown disease. To make matters worse, some medical experts expect that number to double each year. Joining the ranks of those contracting AIDS virus infection are people of all ages, including children, from a variety of backgrounds. What began as a problem predominantly isolated to the male homosexual community, has now broken through into all spheres of society.

There is still much we need to learn about the AIDS virus, but what is known at present is that there are basically three ways a person can become infected. A man or woman may become infected through sexual contact with an infected person. This makes the disease a threat to any person involved in sexual activity with someone who has had more than one sexual partner.

Intravenous drug-users are known to be a high risk group because of syringe sharing. Hospital staff members have expressed concern because they are placed at risk through accidents involving infected blood. There have been cases where recipients of blood transfusions have become infected because the HIV virus was undetected in blood supplies.

Then, sadly, there are the babies born to infected women. Of the million children born to HIV-infected women, about a quarter of them will become infected and most will die of AIDS. The remaining 750,000 will have lost, or can expect to lose, one or both parents to AIDS.[18]

It is vital that we all have at least a basic understanding of what AIDS is and how it works on the human body. Without this knowledge our responses to the AIDS sufferer will be inadequate and we will not be in a strong position to help young people avoid this gruesome disease.

How AIDS Kills

In the first stage of infection the individual shows no signs of having the disease. In fact, the person may appear in good health for a number of years while carrying the virus. Behind the scenes, however, the AIDS virus infiltrates the eyes, brain, lungs, liver, spleen, kidneys and other organs of infected persons.

Infected persons who have not yet developed symptoms are able to transmit the virus to others through various bodily secretions. Every individual who has become infected remains so for the rest of his or her life. There is no way of becoming 'disinfected'. Even if the infected person is not aware of the presence of the virus in his or her body, each person they engage with in intimate sexual activity is also endangered.

The second stage of AIDS infection occurs when an infected person begins to manifest symptoms. These can include sudden unexplained weight loss, drenching night sweats, persistent diarrohea, swelling of the lymph nodes in the armpits and groin, chronic fatigue and/or psychogenic disturbance. The correct name for this condition is 'AIDS related complex (ARC)' and people who develop ARC are critically infected with the AIDS virus.

As the AIDS virus begins to destroy cells in the brain and central nervous system, signs of neurological complications develop. These may include the loss of memory, muscular control and the ability to speak coherently. AIDS-induced brain disease is irreversible.

The number of persons with ARC is estimated by some researchers to be ten times the number of 'full-blown' AIDS cases. Exact numbers of people who have developed ARC are not known. Nevertheless they are capable of transmitting the AIDS virus to others.

Stage three in the development of AIDS is often referred to as 'full-blown' AIDS. It is characterised by severe immune suppression – the wearing away of the body's ability to fight off infections. This is what gives the virus its proper name: Acquired Immune Deficiency Syndrome.

The person who, during the second stage of infection, developed certain physical and mental disorders, is now beset by other diseases called 'opportunistic' infections. These attack when the breakdown of the immune system leaves the body vulnerable. Such diseases include forms of pneumonia, skin cancer, herpes and fungal infection.

Gene Antonio writes that: 'The survival prospects for those who move on to stage three of AIDS virus infection are extremely poor. More than half of those initially diagnosed with full-blown AIDS will be dead in 18 months; more than 70% will be dead within two years. Virtually no-one who has developed the syndrome was alive five years later.'[19] Full-blown AIDS is terminal.

For people who develop immune deficiency, the average time from initial infection to development of symptoms can vary from several weeks to five years or more. The incubation period for AIDS-induced brain disease could range from two to 30 years. Because the adverse effects of AIDS infection can take many years to become manifest, it has a far greater capacity for rapid spread than any of the previous epidemics which have devastated large sections of humanity.

Is God Getting Even?

If we are to steer young friends out of the path of diseases such as AIDS, we need to be informed on those diseases. We also need to formulate the right-responses to young people who have fallen victim to AIDS so that we are able to offer them assistance, or at least understanding.

Some Christians have responded to the whole AIDS problem with claims that AIDS is God's way of evening up the stakes. AIDS, they claim, is the judgement of God on homosexuals and the sexually promiscuous. God's order involves men and women committing themselves to one another in marriage relationships and thereafter experiencing all the joys of sex—with one partner of the opposite sex. However, to say that it is God who inflicts AIDS on people reflects a callous and unjust view of His nature.

How disastrous it would be for us all if God did respond in this way to human sinfulness: 'Let's face it, if God punished sin in this way, the entire population would be dodging thunderbolts 24-hours-a-day, tripping over those struck dead . . . '[20]

Judgement will come—not just for the promiscuous but for all mankind. God will not only judge what we consider to be 'big' sins—even 'small' sins such as lust and greed will be exposed. Also, when God judges, He will not be arbitrary or indiscriminating in His dealings. The AIDS virus is clearly affecting innocent bystanders.

A truly Christian response is a Christ-like one. Caring for the 'untouchable' was always Jesus' way. Modern lepers need the compassionate touch no less than those of ancient times, even those lepers whose own behaviour has been the cause of their problems. Of course, Jesus did not simply overlook the sins of people around Him. But He did offer hope for their future. It was this hope and Jesus' compassion which turned them around morally.

Where Have All The Flowers Gone?

The folk song of this title mourned the death of a generation of young men who went off to war. The flower of youth is cut off in war, and with it the hope and vitality of a nation. Emptiness and despair are left behind.

In a similar way, our modern society has been producing many young people for whom the flowers of youthful dreams, hope and a zest for life have withered. By abandoning moral absolutes we have declared war on our own youth.

So many people abdicate the rights and responsibilities of thinking for themselves on moral issues, choosing instead the less costly route of simply following the crowd and 'moving with the times'. Some presume that we can avoid working through difficult issues, simply by electing governments who will suggest and implement the most moral courses of action. Today's governments, however, are having trouble tackling the social and ethical implications of in-vitro fertilisation, abortion pills, euthanasia and a host of other pressing issues.

The frailty of governments on moral questions simply reflects our own frailty as individual human beings. We need a higher point of reference to which we can turn. Is there such an authority? Is there some 'manufacturer's instruction manual for the human machine'?

I believe there is. Our Maker has made known so much about the human condition. He has provided sensible guidelines for day-to-day living. He has told us how to develop healthy relationships, how to build a happy and secure marriage and home, how to prosper and be content. The Bible deals with more than symptoms. It deals honestly with their root cause, which is separation from God and His plan for our lives. God has dealt with this, the keystone of all our moral problems, through the incarnation, death and resurrection of his Son, Jesus Christ.

If we look honestly and openly at the life of Jesus Christ, I believe, we will discover the greatest humanitarian who ever lived. Jesus taught us that we each have enormous value in God's eyes, and that there is dignity in being God's offspring. But he also saw the great flaws in our psyche which have resulted from our fall from grace. He taught us not to rely on our own concepts of what is right and wrong. He reaffirmed instead the importance of absolutes which have their origin and basis in God.

The so-named Sermon on the Mount is perhaps the fullest, yet most succinct and practical outline ever presented on morality and ethics. But He also gave us what no-one but the Son of God could give. Through His death on a cross at Calvary he bore the horrible eternal consequences of our individual separation from God. Because He was raised again on the third day, He now lives to enable us to actually meet the high and noble standards God has taught through Him. Christ is alive and His strength and love are to be experienced in our lives here and now.

This is the Christian gospel, or 'good news'. Being Christian is not simply trying, in our own strength, to adhere to a rule of life laid down by a great teacher. It is experiencing daily the divine power needed to help us rise above selfishness to a higher, more noble life.

Once we have allowed His power to change us, we must pass this message on to our youth, providing them not just with sound moral principles which lead to rich living, but with the right reason for moral living—a strong, burning love for the God who is there!

5

No Job ... No Good

Unemployment

We come now to what seems to have become a perennial problem for most western nations. It is a problem which of course affects all age groups in society, but is particularly cruel to the young.

Since 1979, the total number of Australians out of work at the start of each year has regularly exceeded the total of 480,000 unemployed during the whole of the great depression of the 1930s. Because the problem just goes on and on, year after year, we tend to grow numb to the pain of others' unemployment. We are anaesthetised into accepting high and rising levels of unemployment as a fact of life, by the conversion of this human crisis into a set of abstract statistics. Keith Windschuttle, a writer on the unemployment problem, says: 'We forget what it is we are measuring. We forget that these numbers are merely abstractions for the lives of real people; that what is being measured is the destination of career, skills, hopes, self-esteem, family relations and the dignity of individual human beings.'[1]

While hopeful politicians have promised a substantial

improvement through better economic management and use of our resources, the fact remains that we have lived with unacceptably high levels of unemployment since the mid-'70s. Since that time, there have been a few mild recoveries at different points but these only managed to hold unemployment at a plateau. We have not seen great reductions in the numbers of people without work.

This problem is, of course, not isolated to one panicular nation. It is a global problem. According to the International Labour Organisation, 36 million people will enter the international labour force every year between now and the year 2,000. The growing magnitude of the problem becomes clear when we consider that, for the entire period 1950 to 1975, there were 22 million people looking for jobs.[2] In his book, *The Lean Years*, Richard J. Barnet states: 'About 85% of the people seeking employment at the dawn of the new century will be in the Third World—well over one billion men and women. To employ them, the Global Factory, the remaining farms, and the growing service economy will have to come up with 120,000 new jobs a day.'[3]

For Keith Windshuttle: 'the only realistic position to take is scepticism . . . We are now well-entrenched within a long economic trough which will see us . . . well into the 1990s. There will be mild upswings within a long economic trough, but these will be insufficient to turn unemployment around to any marked extent. The downswings within the trough will make the dole queues lengthen progressively.'[4]

How must the people involved be feeling, when even the experts see little hope of change to their unemployment woes?

Unemployment can have devastating effects on young people. It directly affects their self-esteem and their sense of hope and purpose for the future. Many are also hurt by the disruption unemployment can cause in their life at home, especially when a parent is without work.

When I was your age . . .

The importance of a healthy self-esteem to any human being cannot be denied. It is not difficult to see how long-term unemployment can whittle away at a young person's self-esteem. Imagine, for example, the effect of parents who are constantly nagging a teenager about his or her lack of a permanent job. 'I left school at 14,' Dad is forever reminding his kids. 'I worked hard and made something of myself. I didn't sit around bludging off others! Why can't you be the same; what's wrong with this generation?'

The fact is, not every young person today can get a job immediately they leave school. (Even a university degree no longer represents a job ticket!) It is not their fault, yet somehow it can leave the young feeling worthless. Life can begin to seem panicularly bleak if, at the same time, they are facing other threats to their self-assurance, such as strained home relationships, broken boy-girl relationships and the like.

If it is not dad and mum who are applying the heat, it is society at large. Even now in the community there exists an antipathy toward the unemployed. There is a certain amount of compassion, but it is tempered with suspicion. The stigma of unemployment means that young people can be assumed guilty of laziness until proven innocent. The media have sometimes added fuel to this fire, by perpetuating negative stereotypes of youth. A young person made the following incisive comment in a letter to a major Australian newspaper: 'If a reader is to pay any attention to the media's opinion of teenagers, the reader would find that teenagers, even when appropriately licensed, are incapable of driving safely at night. The reader would also discover that when teenagers are not drunk or on drugs, we waste our time in other ways. For example, we are all supposedly cheating our way through high school or we are happily unemployed.'[5]

The young unemployed person can also face considerable pressure from his or her peers. Friends who have jobs do not share the burden of long, unproductive days and can exert a subtle but strong pressure by virtue of their ability to buy things. Among males, for example, ownership of a car is still very much a status symbol. Often, a young man's position in the pecking order of the peer group, his ability to command the respect of other young men and to feel that he is attractive to girls, is linked with the state of his automobile. It was Charles Cooley, the social scientist, who told us that a person's self-concept is established by their perception of what the most important people in their lives think of them. The peer group can make material luxuries look like absolute necessities, and without adequate funds young adults may feel their social standing slipping within the group that matters most to them.

For the unemployed, however—and the long-term unemployed in particular—mere necessities often suck up the available funds, leaving precious little for buying status! Michelle Tumer's book, *Stuck*, features a number of revealing interviews with unemployed young people. In one conversation, a young woman has this to say on what it means to be living on the economic knife edge:

'I was on the dole then but that was not enough. I was only getting $36 a week. My board was $20 a week and my food was ten and then there was gas, electricity, etc. So that was just all taken up to eat and to live. I couldn't go out or buy anything like clothes. Little things like shampoo, or toilet paper were a struggle to buy till I got the extra job. Then I was able to buy a little heater for my room.'[6]

The social impact of this kind of lifestyle is evident in the words of an 18-year-old unemployed man: 'When you haven't got the money, you stay at home. Everything virtually slows down . . . phone calls, if you haven't got 30 cents, you can't afford phone calls. That's when you can't go out with your friends. Or put in for petrol. So I virtually "veg" at home . . . '[7]

You may be wondering what the parents and families of these people are doing while all this is happening. Not unexpectedly, studies have shown that there is now a clear link between youth homelessness and unemployment. Many unemployed young people do not receive any form of emotional or practical support from their families. Without this support, and unable to find work, they drift into homelessness.

The results of one study showed that: 'A very high proportion of homeless young people came from broken or unstable families. Mostly these young people were between 15 and 18 years; had little education, low confidence and self-esteem; were carrying personal problems arising from family relationships (or abuse), drugs/alcohol, criminal records and unemployment.'[8]

The effect of unemployment on self-worth is summed

up well in these words from a psychiatrist and family therapist: 'If you're unemployed and all you do is walk down to the front gate and get the paper, go to the unemployment office to look for a job, play guitar and watch TV at the end of the day, you feel unfulfilled and miserable, not worth much as a human being.'[9]

Boring!

If we wanted one word to describe the overall effects of unemployment on the young, the word would have to be boredom! I have watched at times as previously alert and motivated young people have gradually slipped into the boredom mode, often having been without work for quite a while. They have become listless and disinterested in life generally. In some cases they have begun to despair of ever finding a job and building a worthwhile future.

There is a body of evidence now, both in Australia and overseas, to support the contention that unemployment begets unemployment. Many young people who are out of work will have very little chance of ever obtaining a long-term position. There are several reasons for this, not the least of which is that employers, when faced with the choice between hiring someone who has been unemployed for a period of time and someone else who has been in regular employment, will most often hire the latter. There is also the perception among some employers that most unemployed people are not really trying to get work, that they are happy to live off social security benefits.

The lower down the socio-economic scale a young person is, the greater will be the chances that he or she will stay within the spiral of unemployment. Catherine Blakers writes: 'These young people are neither the "bludgers" nor "no-hopers". They are the same kinds [sic] of young people as those who, in the 1950s, 1960s and early 1970s, left school as soon as they could, got jobs, had their youthful flings, got married, bought houses and brought up families. They were the lucky generations in the lucky country. Their children and grandchildren face a bleaker future.'[10]

Today, early school-leavers are at a distinct disadvantage, despite the fact that their fathers and mothers may have done quite well taking that same path. Employers invariably look for skills and experience, personal confidence and problem-solving capacities, and a generally high level and quality of education. Those who must leave school early, either because their families cannot afford to keep them on, or because the home environment is not supportive of study habits, will find it difficult to compete.

As long ago as 1939, an unemployed 19-year-old was feeling this despair: 'How the youth of today longs for something to do: an odd job now and then is little help, accompanied as it is by the fear of what is to come next week. Like the statue, the youth overlooks a world in which he can take no part, can achieve nothing.'[11] The thoughts of a more contemporary teenager express these same sentiments: 'As the months get along you just get more depressed. And you feel as if you're a no-hoper, you're nothing. You don't really count anywhere, you don't belong anywhere . . . What's the use of even existing. You're just some statistic . . . or something.'[12]

Keith Windshuttle sums up the situation well, when he says that we are producing, 'a hard core of young people who are now moving into their twenties with a background of long-term unemployment punctuated by brief periods of casual, unskilled and often part-time labour . . . We are producing a sizeable majority of young people who are condemned to inhabit the marginal regions of the labour market for the rest of their lives. In an economy that is progressively shedding its demand for unskilled labour, the long-term prospect for these people is especially bleak.'[13]

Young people need challenge. They are built for adventure. Doing interesting, new and productive things helps them establish their identity. In the minds of many teenagers, who have been cheated of parental encouragement and recognition of their achievements over the years, leaving school and finding a job may offer the last great opportunity to feel productive. They may see employment as their means of at last establishing their niche in the world. When they find no job awaiting them, they may, over a period of time, grow increasingly frustrated, disillusioned and then angry with the system, especially when it does not seem to care about their predicament.

Unemployment is a situation many feel powerless to change. With powerlessness comes frustration and anger. Many young people feel this way when confronted by seeming hopeless situations, and bureaucracies which don't bend over backwards to help. Cornered and surrounded by pressures such as unemployment and despair, so many store away negative feelings until these are given vent in behaviour that is anti-social or anti-self.

Many young people turn their anger inwards, sinking into the mire of self-loathing. Eventually the potential they do possess is buried under layer upon layer of self-hatred. There are now clearly established links between unemployment and suicide. In the UK, for example, suicide rates have increased by 3% each year since 1975, reversing a downward trend in the '60s. Suicides there are most common among young males in the lowest socio-economic group—the class which is most vulnerable to unemployment[14]. In Australia, some studies have been undertaken into this area and, from the analysis which is currently available, it seems that 'unemployment is likely to be a factor in the recent rise in suicide of men between 20 and 24 because the largest increase is found in areas associated with the manufacturing industry.'[15]

The other potential and often-realised scenario is that, faced with little prospect of gainful employment, young people may vent their anger on the community at large. A combination of boredom and frustration leads many to crime. To illustrate this point, I read of a police charge sheet from a suburban police station in Adelaide, South Australia, where, of the 29 youths (aged 15 to 25 years) charged during one week in October, 70% were unemployed. Three of the charges were for robbery or property offences and three were for assault. The remainder were for drug, speeding or loitering offences[16].

Michelle Turner feels that, 'Denying some people a sense of self-worth and locking them out of the economic good life by tolerating high levels of unemployment invites anti-social behaviour. There is also a vicious circle for the offender. Once convicted he becomes a recognised "outsider", the police "record" making it even harder to get employment.'[17]

With little possibility of building a career which provides opportunities for productivity and creativity many young people give in to despair.

Unemployment also affects young people through the breakdown of their families. The statistical evidence is clear: the effects on families with fathers who are unemployed are devastating. Unemployment is directly linked to increases in separation, divorce, domestic violence and psychological breakdown. Even if they have jobs themselves, young people may be made to suffer through the idleness of other members of their families. They may be gravely hurt by unemployment even before they are old enough to work.

'They didn't teach us how to live!'

The whole youth unemployment problem is compounded by the failure of many parents and educationalists to equip young people for life itself. American educationalist Herbert Kohl has identified five essentials for citizenship in a democratic society. They are listed below. As you read them, consider carefully whether the young people coming out of our homes and schools today are being fitted with these important tools:

1. The ability to use language well and thoughtfully.
2. The ability to think through a problem and experiment with solutions.
3. The ability to understand scientific and technological ideas and to use tools.
4. The ability to understand how people function in groups.
5. The ability to know how to learn something yourself.[18]

So many of the young today are being robbed of the training in basic life skills they so desperately need, if they are to successfully negotiate life in our complex and fast-changing world. Many school leavers today— even those who complete a full secondary school programme—display very poor reading and communication skills. Yet we expect them to make a success of themselves in a world that is information crazy!

The full volume of human knowledge continues to expand at an incredible rate, making each new book that is printed represent a smaller and smaller fraction of all that is known to man. Ideas come and go, theories change and new discoveries are commonplace. In Shakespeare's day there were around 200,000 usable words in the English language. Now there are over 450,000, which means that if Bill the Bard turned up on the main streets of one of our cities today, he would be semi-literate! Terms such as 'nuclear spillage,' 'forest shrinkage' and 'ozone depletion' were largely unheard of just a few years ago. Yet today they are commonplace, and each represents a large body of ideas, issues and debates.

Alvin Toffler called all this the 'rapid obsolescence of knowledge' and suggested that, as we continue to create and use up ideas and images at an increasingly fast pace, knowledge becomes 'disposable' just like the household items we se briefly and throw away. In the quest for meaning in life, people today are hooked on ideas, and society demands that we each be able to communicate clearly the flow of ideas around us. For so many of our youth the world of ideas is a foreign one. They have not been equipped to pick up new concepts and expand their base of knowledge.

As a society, we do tend to expect a great deal from our schools—perhaps a little too much at times. As with any other large human institution which has been around for a while, the school system is slow to change, especially when its traditions and patterns have been accepted for over 200 hundred years. Pressures on the schools are exerted from all sides, and not all the criticisms levelled against the system are valid. However, it is becoming clearer by the day, that traditional forms of education do not necessarily meet the needs of non-traditional, technology-based industries. There is much talk among employers, parents and teachers at present, about how the system needs to change in order to better equip the young and serve industry. Catherine Blakers sums up the situation: 'Up to the present the society and its schools have muddled along in the expectation that, when the economy righted itself, both social and educational problems would subside. Now the society has begun to realise that it is faced with fundamental change, and the schools, and education generally, have been thrust into the battle for economic survival.'[19]

In the past, we have assumed that the role of the individual in our society will remain more or less static, and that the education required for that role will need little alteration in the individual's lifetime. Any changes that may be required will be successfully negotiated via experience and ad-hoc arrangements. But the kind of society we live in today is far from static; we live in a storm of change. Now, many different interest groups agree that changes must be made in the schooling given our kids, but the directions that change should take are, as yet, far from clear. I think we can say that today's kids need to be taught basic principles and disciplines in the types of subjects which most previous generations have taken for granted. But they also need to gain perspectives on problem solving, team work, adapting to new technologies and interpersonal relationships. Many teenagers and young adults have little understanding of how to face and work through problems, and how to discern what is truth in a matter. Instead of teaching them problem solving procedures, many parents have either over-protected their children, never allowing them to solve problems on their own, or have simply assumed that they instinctively know how to muddle through.

The ability to think rationally through a problem is, in part, handed down to us via the DNA package we receive at conception. But this innate rationality must be finetuned through training. Children need a certain amount of training in identifying the real root problem in a given situation; in how to identify their available options for response; and in how to choose and follow the most fruitful course of action. They also need to be supported as they work through this process time and time again, until they achieve a level of independence in solving problems.

Also, the young need to be taught how to think for themselves so that they can form their own views on the flood tide of media messages with which they are being bombarded. We receive, through our sophisticated media systems, carefully trimmed, edited and stream-lined messages. Someone in the production or editorial team decides what will be aired, or printed, and what will be omitted. In order to attract viewers, and sponsor-ship dollars, even so-called responsible TV current affairs programmes will sometimes resort to cheap sensationalism. As a result, issues are blurred by emotionalism, and perceptions are sometimes coloured by biased editing.

There are, of course, some fine, caring and responsible people within our media organisations. But the system in which they work is one which can can powerfully in-fluence our perceptions of what is happening in the world.

Our youth need training in how to discern truth for

themselves. As we've already seen, when the young become frustrated by events they don't understand, or come to believe that they have none of the muscle to improve things, the results can be fairly destructive.

To put responsibility for teaching all this back wholly onto the schools is, of course, unfair and unrealistic. The part parents can play is not to be underestimated and they will need to be more involved. There will also need to be much more training in the work place provided, or at least facilitated and encouraged, by employers. We will need to change the perception that 'vocational education' is not 'real' education. We may also need to adjust our preference for academic training over trade skills, if we are to ensure that the young are exposed to training which will actually mean something in the world of tomorrow.

Whatever forms it takes, education needs to be related to real needs, and ongoing throughout life. As Blakers so aptly puts it, 'education is no longer a matter of an initial dose that does you lasting good.'[20]

6

Nobody's Hero

Challenge And Despair

Australian singer John Farnham had a hit with a song called *You're The Voice.*

It caught on like a bushfire around the nation because it struck a chord in the hearts of millions of young record buyers. It is a song about heroism, about standing up and being counted, about getting involved. It tells the young that they are significant in their world. They have power to change society for the better; they can make a difference if they let their voice be heard.

This is a message kids are longing to hear. In his Pulitzer prize-winning book, *Denial Of Death,* Ernest Becker puts forward the idea that mankind's greatest fear is the fear of death. In the face of death, a man or woman will seek to gain some kind of immortality—to stretch their influence beyond the natural limitations of time—by doing something which will live on after they are gone. By doing something important with their lives, says Becker, people are seeking a significance in history.[1]

Young people especially are built for heroism. The young thirst for adventure. They crave recognition and love, and if these can only be bought with heroics, then heroes they will seek to be.

The United Nations has estimated that 200,000 children under the age of 15 are bearing arms around the world in wars of various kinds. At no more than 12 years of age, boys are going off to war, fighting for causes they don't understand or won't live long enough to see fulfilled. In Afghanistan, Northern Ireland, Israel, Myanmar (formerly Burma) and even Los Angeles, kids are fighting for something; fighting with real weapons against real enemies.[2]

In less troubled parts of the world, young people satisfy their taste for adventure in other ways. Often, they look for it in cinemas or concert venues. Here, lives without drama are soon packed with non-stop action, through the power of imagination. Adventures are lived out vicariously through screen heroes or pop idols.

In one survey in the US, 70% of teenagers aged between 14 and 17 years claimed that they went to the movies primarily to find a hero. Screen and music idols have taken on a whole new significance for the kids of the affluent baby-boomer generation. An Australian study has shown that only 8% of teenagers in this country consider their father or mother to be among their key role models. Most name celebrities as the major shaping influences in their lives.[3]

Perhaps this is partly because, while they gladly embrace the benefits of their parents' materialistic lifestyle, young people are also aware that it's not enough to satisfy the human soul. According to a Gallup International poll, conducted among 40,000 people in 20 countries, Australians are among the 'most satisfied people in the world, but also rate among the most bored and lonely.'[4]

Don't Worry Be Happy

One song which captured the hearts of Australians when it was first released, was a little number called simply, *Don't Worry Be Happy*. A tune about laying back and enjoying life in the midst of life's knocks, it stayed on or near the top of the charts for quite some time in most parts of Australia. It related to the hopes and aspirations of everyday people. If you were to ask the average man-in-the-street what he wanted for himself, his wife and his family, he would probably answer something like this: 'I just want us to be happy.' Yet so few people in the country which was once called the 'land of plenty' ever seem to find contentment and happiness.

Why is this? Perhaps it's partly because we have an inadequate concept of what constitutes true happiness. Jesus Christ had some interesting things to say about happiness. According to Jesus, it is the poor in spirit, those who acknowledge that they have a need, who find happiness. He said that those who mourn, those who are meek and those who show mercy are the ones who really discover its secrets. He even went as far as to state that happiness belongs to those who are persecuted (Matthew 5:3-12)!

On the surface it doesn't sound as if Jesus of Nazareth knew very much about happiness at all! Surely it's not the needy, but those who have everything they require who are happy. We all know, don't we, that those who mourn are unhappy and that the meek will always be far less content than those who have power? It is the popular, not the persecuted, who live happily ever after.

Could the great teacher have been so far off base? Actually, I think there's more here than meets the eye. I think Jesus is trying to tell us that our idea of happiness is founded on a wrong premise. We live as if happiness

is a state of mind we will achieve when we have disposed
of all our problems. Some people spend a good deal of
money on chemical substances which provide a short
escape from life's problems. Others turn to entertainment of one form or another for their escape.

According to Jesus, though, happiness is sometimes to
be found in the midst of trial. There is a kind of
fulfillment to be found even in situations which make us
feel powerless, or cause us to weep over our need, or
result in our being ostracised from the crowd. This
happiness is not based on the 'me first' principle. It comes
to those who, even in their hard times, try to turn their
trials into something of benefit—for themselves and for
other people.

The other significant thing Jesus is telling us is that the
priority we give happiness is unhealthy. Not only have
we defined it badly, we've also made it our god. It's our
goal, the thing we live and work for. God did not
intend happiness to be our goal, though. We were built
for a higher goal. We were made to be significant and
it's only when we reach out to achieve God's plan for
our lives that we discover what it means to be truly
happy. Happiness, contentment, is a place we pass
through on our way to a higher destination.

Martin Luther King made this observation: 'An
individual has not started living until he can rise above
the narrow confines of his individualistic concerns to the
broader concerns of all humanity . . . Every man must
decide whether he will walk in the light of creative
altruism or the darkness of destructive selfishness . . .
Life's most persistent and urgent question is, "What are
you doing for others?" '5

A friend of mine was killed while ministering in his
homeland of Sri Lanka. Rohan Dissaneyeke had studied

the Bible in New Zealand and felt that God was calling back him to the land of his birth. He and his young Australian wife, Alison, took up an associate pastorate in a major Sri Lankan church. From there he trained and sent out younger men who planted new churches in outlying areas. He was well-known and highly regarded as a church leader and a man of complete sincerity and integrity.

In the process of bringing his church planting dreams into reality he began to work among people in the north east of the country, in areas where tensions had given rise to violence between the two major Sri Lankan racial groups. The Tamils—whose ancestry is Indian—were seeking to set up an independent state in this area. The Singhalese population—descended from the original Ceylonese people—vehemently resisted this idea in the national parliament, where they held a majority. The result was a state of affairs bordering on civil war. Innocent people were being killed and this beautiful country's economic survival was placed under threat.

Rohan put aside thoughts of personal comfort. His burden of compassion for the needy people of the north far outweighed any concerns for personal safety. He started an outreach programme, regularly travelling north with young proteges who were eager to assist. One evening, as their van made its way through winding village streets, they were ambushed by a group of armed guerillas. Rohan and several friends were killed in cold blood. He was not a soldier and he carried no banner for either side of the confiict. Neither he nor his Bible students were politically aligned. His only interest was helping the innocent people who were suffering in the carnage.

I saw my friend Rohan just weeks before he died. We

spoke and prayed together at a church leaders' conference in Brisbane. I'll never forget the broad, open smile he wore when we parted. Strangely, despite the difficulties he knew he might face on his return to Sri Lanka, he struck me as being a very happy man. He spoke enthusiastically about his plans and dreams even though his eyes were wide open to the possible dangers. It seemed that Rohan had tapped the well-spring of real happiness, without having made it his main pursuit.

Another friend of mine is a police officer in Belfast, Northern Ireland. He is a committed Christian and has watched the tragedy of Northern Ireland's troubles unfold around him, bringing grief and despair to the lives of friends and colleagues.

He is required by law to carry a gun with him at all times. If he should decide that he does not want to wear his gun to church, his wife must carry it in her handbag. It's very encouraging driving in his car—before you get in he must check to see that it's not wired for explosives. Staying with him is both a joy and a challenge, for he runs his hands around the front door jambs before unlocking it, again checking that no unwelcome visitor has entered to leave an explodable brown paper parcel inside.

I came to love this man and his beautiful family. When I first met them, I was deeply impressed by their warmth and joviality. I asked my friend why he remained in this powderkeg environment, why he didn't apply to emigrate to Australia, or Canada, or anywhere that offered a more peaceful and certain way of life. His reply touched me with its sincerity. 'Mal, I would leave tomorrow,' he said, 'if it wasn't for the fact that this is where God has called me to be. I have such a burden for my people.'

This is a family bound together both by the troubles around them and by their common commitment to serving Christ in the situation. Just as Martin Luther King and Rohan Dissaneyeke did, they are pursuing higher goals and in the process discovering meaning. By example, we must teach young people this radical approach to happiness.

Power To The People

There are indications that some young people, in their quest for significance and adventure, have turned to religious cults and even the occult. Eben Durrant, whose story was outlined in chapter two, is an example of a teenager whose search for identity led him to dabble with Satanism. His involvement with satanic groups, and a fixation with the idea of death, ended in his tragic suicide.

Satanism is the antithesis of Christianity and is founded on the belief that Satan can offer a person power through indulgence in vices derived from man's animal nature. Selfishness, vengeance and personal power are its cornerstones. In the United States, where reports linking murders and suicides with occultism have existed for some years, the indications are that young people involve themselves in Satanism in order to achieve some kind of personal power. They are often attracted by the promise of magical powers which are supposedly achieved through a pact with the devil.

Some young people who become deeply involved in occultism come to believe that killing themselves, then others, is the ultimate thing they can do in satanic worship. In their minds, they believe they will come back as more powerful beings because of these acts of tribute to Satan. In West Virginia a 13-year-old girl shot her father to death while he slept. In Missouri three teenagers beat a classmate to death then dumped him in a sewer along with the carcass of a bludgeoned cat. In New Jersey a 13-year-old boy scout killed and mutilated his mother in a horror frenzy. All three crimes were committed in the name of the devil.

In the US, certain patterns have emerged regarding the type of young person who is becoming involved in Satanism. He or she is apparently most often an intelligent person, sometimes an underachiever, and usually from a middle or upper class background. Such patterns are to be found in other western nations, including Australia. Boredom and inferiority are clearly factors which influence some relatively affluent young people toward occultism.

No Antidote For Blues?

Dire Straits spoke for many young people when they wrote and sang: 'I can't find no antidote for blues.'

When personal identity and meaning become hard to find, despair often creeps in, uninvited, to fill the vacuum. For many young people today, despair is simply a part of life.

After speaking with a cross section of Australian young people, social researcher Hugh Mackay found that many are pessimistic, possessing a 'vague sense of impending disaster.'[6] He found that today's young Australians regard instability as a fact of life.

Richard Eckersley, author of the Commission for the Future report, *Casualties of change: the predicament of youth in Australia*, summarises the pressures faced by young people throughout the developed world: 'Pressures of increasing urbanisation, industrialisation, centralisation, mechanisation, individualism; of growing populations, increasing global economic competition and accelerating change; of a strengthening material and economic domination of our lives and a weakening spiritual and moral influence; of the development and employment of ever more powerful and complex technologies that diminish the individual's place in society and sense of control over his or her destiny.[7]

Alvin Toffler wrote in *Future Shock* of what he called the 'age of impermanence' and the 'roaring current of change', correctly postulating that the rate of change in modern times would lead increasingly to a problem of identity for the individual. Young people are the ones at the forefront of all this rapid change. The average family in most developed western societies moves house once every three or four years. Children have little time to put down roots and form lasting relationships. They often grow up having had no opportunity to establish a sense of geographical or relational 'location' for themselves.

The young today also live in an increasingly depersonalised society. This is the 'please let me be somebody' generation. Teenagers often need to compete for attention and affection in the home and beyond. Many government organisations which were set up to help young people, have grown into institutional monsters. As teenagers leave home they must begin the struggle to keep their dignity in the face of systems which treat them more and more as computer numbers and less and less as individuals. All of this contributes to a fairly pessimistic window on life in many young minds.

It should not surprise us, then, to find that many young people are confused about their place in the world, and about what they can do to make any positive personal contribution to its future. Despair sets in when kids simply do not believe that they can make a difference.

Consider the state-wide research done by an assistant director of the South Australian Education Department. He began by asking eight students in a country high school to imagine themselves floating away from the earth and returning in 20 years' time. He asked them to describe what they thought they would see. He was so depressed by the answers that he almost gave up the study. Several hundred students later, he was able to show that those country high schoolers were in fact typical in their outlook.

He found that most teenagers envisage a barren, lifeless world. 'The world seems completely ruined,' wrote one student. 'Nuclear bombs have been dropped recently. I come upon the remnants of a burnt hand. Then four very wrinkled old men. They are a horrible sight. They have burn marks all over their bodies and no hair on their heads. They seem to be searching through the rubble for food.'[8]

So much has been said so often about the possibility of nuclear warfare in our time. An Australian TV documentary described a young boy's efforts to speak with two world leaders on the issue of world peace. He wrote to the then president of the United States, Ronald Reagan, and the leader of the U.S.S.R., Mikhail Gorbachev, seeking an audience with each so that he could present an 11-year-old's perspective on the build up of nuclear arsenals.

The reporter and producers working on the documentary, which was called *Mum, How Do You Spell Gorbatrof?*, applauded this boy's desire to become involved in world affairs. Wasn't it marvellous that a child like this should become so worked up about nuclear issues? they said. For my part, I couldn't help feeling some sadness at the fact that someone so young needed to be thinking about such things at all! When I was his age, I had barely even heard of nuclear weaponry and was much more concerned with football, cars and girls (in that order). It seems that many of our kids can't even be kids any more.

Many young people live consciously or unconsciously with the fear that the nuclear flash might come at some time down the track and wipe out their future altogether. This threat can cause some teenagers, who are already troubled, to wonder whether making a real effort in life is actually worth the trouble. Perhaps they might do just as well to accept the philosophy of someone like John Bonham, the one time musician with Led Zeppelin. I've heard it said that when Bonham was found dead at an early age, he had fulfilled his life motto: 'Live fast and die young.' It is not surprising that, in one Australian survey, 66% of young people agreed that the future is so uncertain that it is best to live from day to day.[9]

There are other issues which, to young people, also make the future seem bleak. How often can teenagers hear that America is in debt, that Mexico is bankrupt, and that other countries cannot afford to repay even the interest on their loans from world banks, before they begin to wonder how, if nations cannot make ends meet financially, they're going to manage their accounts?

Many of the lobby groups which have taken up crusades on important issues have very good intentions. However, few of them seem to appreciate what a gloomy picture their work, when it is all taken together, is painting for some young people.

We need to present young people with a message of hope and personal significance. We need to reaffirm their responsibility for their actions and the fact that, because their behaviour does have an affect on their surroundings, they have the capacity to change their world for the better. If we fail in this we are surrendering the young to pessimism and despair.

A lack of personal identity and a pessimistic view of the world and its future are a potent mixture. Taken together, they can produce a state of mental anguish and defeatism from which a teenager might never recover. For those who have no sense of purpose, no ability to conceive of a brighter future through the use of their own talents, life can become intolerable.

7

Bang! Bang!
I'm Dead ...

Suicide

Her name was Megan. She was 15 years of age—a
desperately lonely, disillusioned and confused young
lady who, on three occasions, had tried to commit
suicide.

When asked why she had gone to such repeated
lengths to end her life, she told a story of great personal
struggle, of crushing disappointments and frustrations,
of anger with life in general, and of that loneliest of all
feelings—that no-one cared for or understood her. As if
to sum up she added these tragic words: 'In the end life
just seemed like such a waste of time.'[1]

Megan had lost all sense of meaning in life at the
tender age of fifteen! Unfortunately, every year in
Australia there are thousands of young Megans who
attempt suicide. Of these, hundreds succeed, and hundreds feel cheated when they don't. Until 1961, suicide
in this country was a problem mainly relating to older
age groups. Over the past two decades, however, suicide
among young men and women has increased alarmingly.

More than 1600 Australians will commit suicide this

year; more than 350 of these will be under the age of 25 years.[2] It is difficult to estimate the number of unsuccessful attempts at suicide made each year. Authorities variously claim between 50 and 200 attempts for each completed suicide. This means that anywhere between 20,000 and 80,000 young people will attempt to end their own lives this year. (And this is the so-called 'lucky country'!)

This number will not include all those young people whose deaths will be labelled by coroners as 'accidental' or 'cause undetermined' when, in fact, there may have been a deliberate suicide intent. Some car accidents will not be accidents and some 'accidental' drug overdoses will be deliberate. Unless a suicide note is found in such cases, or a list of previous suicide attempts or threats exists, a death will not be labelled a suicide. The actual number of completed suicides will be even higher than the best official records show.

In Australia, suicide is now the second biggest killer of males aged between 15 and 24 years. Only road accidents claim the lives of more of our young men. Young men are more likely to use violent methods such as shooting and hanging; young women are more likely to poison themselves, by overdosing on prescription drugs.[3]

While suicide among boys aged 15 to 19 years has doubled in the past 20 years, and is still up to five times greater than for girls, the rate of suicide among our young women increased by 50% in 3 years during the 1980s. Both young men and women are suffering in our society and the youth suicide problem has reached proportions that ought to concern everyone. According to a survey conducted in schools in the Hornsby area near Sydney, in every class of 30 students, two students aged between 12 and 16 years are potentially suicidal. Suicide rates for even the five to 14 years age group have risen markedly in recent years.

Suicide has overtaken cancer in our child death statistics, according to a five year research programme completed for the Western Australian Health Department. While we are justifiably spending large amounts of money, time and resources trying to tackle killer diseases such as cancer, most of us are not well informed about the rising menace of youth suicide. It is a sad fact that, in many instances, we seem to be able to do little to save young cancer victims. But the problem of youth suicide is one that we can alleviate—if we'll just stir ourselves and become involved. Young people from all socio-economic groups are affected—people of various races; people from country centres as well as large cities.

Fortunately, there are common factors involved in the plight of most young would-be suiciders, and common early warning signs tell us that a person's problems are becoming unmanageable for them. By observing these warning signs, we are able to save precious lives. For those who wish to help, there are practical things which can be done. For those who are feeling overpowered by life's problems and are contemplating suicide, there is hope for a better life ahead.

Suicide: Destruction or Escape?

There are various views espoused today on what suicide is. Not everybody feels the same way about the issue. Obviously our approach to this question will greatly affect our views on what should be done with someone who is in a potentially suicidal state.

Some people in our society are portraying suicide as a legitimate way for an individual to exercise control over his or her life. According to these people, among them quite a number of humanist writers, suicide is no more than the individual's exercising of his or her right to end life when and how he or she chooses to. One such writer called suicide 'the signature of freedom'.

An internationally renowned current affairs magazine carried an article entitled A Deliberate Date with Death. The article described how a former chief of the Reserve Bank of Australia and his wife, both 75 years of age, had each taken an overdose of tablets and died together in their flat near Sydney. They were in a very good position financially and were both physically active and in good health. Each enjoyed hobbies and interests outside of their home. Yet they had made a pact to die together and had planned and scheduled the event some time in advance. The article describes the reaction of their family: 'The family said the decision had been taken in a spirit of serenity and contentment and we love and respect them for it.'[4]

Sadly, such sentiments about suicide are leaving a whole generation of young people, whose lives have hardly begun, with a view that suicide is a legitimate and acceptable way to die. Instead of giving our youth models of resilience, creativity and determination with which to face problems, we are offering them a kind of voluntary euthanasia. This devaluation of human life is nothing less than a crime perpetrated against the young people of this nation. Too many young people are seeing suicide as a way out. As a society we have, in some ways, let down our guard on suicide, and it's the young who are collecting the fatal body blows!

Many people, who in some troubled time earlier in their lives attempted suicide, will today tell you that they are glad they failed—that life has turned out to be better than they had anticipated. Too many young people are not getting a chance to find that out, largely because some have made death by suicide seem better than living. Problems are temporary, they can be managed if not solved. Suicide, on the other hand, is permanent.

Someone has described suicide as 'a deadly act of violence directed against self.' It is often the case that troubled people who have no-one to turn to, vent their anger on themselves. They allow anger and frustration to build up inside them, until they begin to see themselves as the cause of all their problems. Self-hatred is often a characteristic of those who attempt suicide.

Another writer has called suicide 'the ultimate disconnection'—the ultimate escape from life's puzzles and problems. To a young person whose family and general environment have never equipped him or her with problem-solving or conflict management skills, suicide can appear to be the only realistic option.

Sadly, many young people today are surrounded by elders who themselves seek refuge in a bottle, a medicine cabinet or an extra-marital relationship. The teenager is left to ponder how in the world, if adults can't deal with their hang-ups, inexperienced kids can be expected to deal with theirs!

Traditionally our society has based its views on the sanctity of human life on biblical Christian values. The Christian view is that life is God's gift to mankind. According to the Genesis account, mankind was given a quality of life quite different from that of the animals. Human beings were, it says, created in the likeness of God.

Man has several God-like attributes. He is able to exercise logic and is free to exercise his will (though not free to escape the consequences of bad or wrong decisions), thus providing the right of self-determination. He is also blessed with a great capacity for creativity and carries within him an urge to accomplish something lasting and eternal.

In our age, humanistic evolutionists are insisting—without conclusive scientific evidence—that man is no more than a freak evolutionary accident, 'a monkey who got lucky'. It is refreshing to be reminded again of the Christian belief that mankind was the idea of a creative, benevolent and powerful God. According to the Bible, every man and woman is intended by God to experience life as a thrilling adventure, to dream big dreams and reach worthwhile goals. Then it goes even further, to declare that Jesus Christ, the Son of God, died a horrific death, in order to remove the stain on humanity which resulted from our disobedience of God's directions for life. Each man and woman is valuable because they are the objects of God's love, the recipients of the greatest gift God could give—His Son!

It is not surprising to find, then, that Christians are often at the forefront of campaigns to save human life and dignity. Suicide is the ultimate expression of faithlessness in human value and it runs against the very deep grain of self-preservation within all of us. It is a waste—the sad and untimely end to a life full of potential for good dreams and great deeds.

People who have had someone close to them take their own life will be able to affirm the fact that suicide leaves friends and relatives feeling devastated. Relatives are left to deal with a mixture of anger, guilt and frustration. Friends wonder whether they could have done more to help. One mother whose child committed suicide expressed her feelings this way: 'I'll never feel really happy again,' she said. Human life is valuable. It is to be protected at all costs.

Why suicide?

Most of us know that, even when our problems seem insurmountable, we will somehow muddle through as we have done before. We know that others have come through similar predicaments and we expect to do the same. For this reason, it can be very hard for us to understand just what a young person is going through when they consider suicide as their only solution.

In some cases a young person will attempt suicide as a result of depressive illness—that is, a physiological disorder which can be inherited. In such cases the depression can be treated medically using prescribed drugs to correct a chemical imbalance in some part of the brain. Some people will require hospitalisation for a short space of time. Ongoing support from both doctor and family will often help the sufferer get back into the mainstream of society.

However, depression as associated with suicide is less often a disease than an emotional state, a learned response to external problems. Otherwise mentally sound people can become helplessly bound by strong negative emotions and thoughts. Their highly stressed state can be far more difficult to deal with than depressive illness, as its causes may be many and very complex, and largely beyond the ability of physical science to solve.

Nearly all young people who attempt suicide have feelings of desperation, of being isolated and having no-one with whom they can communicate their needs. In fact, they feel so isolated that, even if there are people around them to whom they can talk, they don't really believe they're getting through. They will try harder and harder to make their feelings known until finally they become desperate, and despair of ever finding a solution.

This kind of depression may be triggered by a number of factors. People generally are experiencing a growing feeling of powerlessness in the face of rapid change. A psychologist studying the attitudes and feelings of middle-class people in several major cities found that: 'Ordinary Australians are deeply concerned about the pace of change in their society. They feel changes are random and uncontrollable. And this perceived lack of control over change produces anxiety and a state of apprehension. Australians believe that change brings with it a lack of control over events and a feeling of powerlessness that they find frightening.'[5]

In an environment of negativity, people feel less able to cope with change and so come to view the future as a threatening thing. This can contribute to severe depression.

There is evidence that people tend to make a sharp distinction between their personal future and the future of society or the world: 'a happy belief that the misfortunes that they believe are increasingly likely to befall others, won't affect them.'[6]

In the US, a survey of more than 600,000 school students found that most believed their personal future would be a prosperous and happy one, whilst their prognosis for the nation and the world was grim. Australian studies also show that young people tend to feel confident that they'll get what they want out of life, despite their reservations about the future of the planet. It seems that personal optimism offers some kind of barrier against the damaging psychological effects of a despairing world view. When this optimism is weakened through adverse personal circumstances—family breakdown, broken relationships and the like—pessimism about the future of the world can be translated into a sense of hopelessness on a personal level.

Serious depression can arise as a result of an individual's continuing sense of failure. Often, the event which actually seems to have triggered a suicide attempt appears trivial to an onlooker. The cat that dies, the friend who says the wrong thing or the bad grade in school—all may simply be the final straw in a long line of perceived failures.

The real problem often begins in childhood. Traumas such as rape, incest or violence experienced in childhood years can return to haunt people in adolescence or even adulthood.

When other present pressures bear down on the already hurting individual it can seem that the whole world is sending them a message—your life is not worth preserving! For young people, the effects of one perceived failure on top of an already insecure sense of personal identity can be devastating. I say 'perceived' failure, because many young people set very unfair standards of performance for themselves.

One bright high school student, on the day she gained a B+ grading in an exam, went home and killed herself with her father's shotgun. This grade was seen by her as a major failure. She had always achieved A's in previous exams; it was what her parents expected of her. They had always made it clear that they wanted the best for her, and expected nothing but the best from her. In the weeks leading up to this, she had been through a whole series of setbacks. Taken separately, these were very small but, strung together in her perfectionist's brain, they took on more significant proportions. Achieving a lower than expected grade was the last straw.

This girl's problem was exacerbated by parents who had unrealistic expectations where their teenager was concerned. Achievement-based love is not love at all. It sets young people up for frustration with themselves. When they feel the need for more love or acceptance, they drive themselves to higher and higher levels of achievement, until finally they feel unable to fulfil the expectations placed upon them.

I have spoken with a number of teenagers who have been told, or led to believe, that they were an 'accident of birth'. This would have to be the most cruel thing a parent can deposit in the mind of their child. It is not really surprising that young people who have grown up believing themselves to be failures in life—no matter how hard they try to do better—should come to the point where they tire of persisting with themselves and attempt suicide.

In chapter one, we looked at the pressures brought to bear on young people as a result of family breakdown. Parents often leave their children vulnerable to severe depression because they provide no firm discipline. Children recognise parental discipline, correctly and fairly given, as a sign of love. Too many parents in recent decades have abandoned their role as disciplinarians in the home, preferring to abdicate this responsibility to schools, churches and other community groups. Consequently when the child 'goes off the rails' in some way, it is—in their eyes—the world at large which is to blame. Teenagers who have never known caring parental discipline often fall prey to depressing feelings that they are unwanted or unworthy of anyone's interest. I will say more on discipline in chapter twelve.

Copycat Suicide

One of the alarming facts to come out of worldwide research into youth suicide, is that suicide seems at times to 'spread' among teenagers like some kind of contagious disease. 'Teen suicide unquestionably is an imitative and contagious phenomenon,' says Dr. H.M. Hoberman, co-director of the suicide and depression clinic at the University of Minnesota Hospital.[7]

Studies have shown that vulnerable young people often feel they are being 'given permission' to commit suicide when they hear that others are doing it. This 'copycat' syndrome is particularly dangerous when an already depressed young person has lost a loved one, especially an adult, to suicide. It has been suggested that the majority of adolescents who take their own lives are children, or close relatives, of people who have either attempted or committed suicide.

In the early part of 1987, four teenagers committed suicide together by shutting themselves into a car in an abandoned garage in Bergenfield, New Jersey, USA, and letting the motor run. Three of them had relatives who had attempted suicide. As if to further illustrate the 'copycat' mentality, two other teenagers attempted to kill themselves in the same town, by the same means, one week later.

I'm excited about being able to share with young people the answers that Jesus Christ gives for life's problems. On hundreds of occasions I have personally watched as boredom, apathy and frustration have given way to a fresh sense of purpose and vigour for living after a young person has prayed to commit their life to Christ and his cause. Make no mistake—there is real supernatural, life-transforming power in the message of salvation the Bible gives us. It is a message modern man needs to hear and act upon. The Christian message is that life can be and should be an adventure, a quest to fulfil God's purpose and plan for our individual lives. Life is therefore worth preserving at all costs. Suicide runs against the very deep grain of self-preservation within all of us.

The Bible gives answers to the dilemmas and traumas facing modern man. There is hope even for a seemingly pointless and unhappy life. Asking God's forgiveness for our rebellious nature and confessing our trust in His Son, Jesus, as our means of salvation opens the door for God to pour His love into our broken lives and reveal to each of us His healing power. This is a very personal thing—an encounter between men and women and their Creator. It is life-changing.

Part Two

Saving The Endangered Species

'PLEASE GOD'

Please God, tell me,
are you Buddhist, Jehovah or
Jew?
What's the colour of your
skin,
black, white, yellow or blue?

Why the blacks in the east
have hollow guts and hungry
eyes,
but we still stuff our face
with yellow cakes to french
fries.

When a gun kills a dozen
in the busy Queen street;
why the banning of guns
should be such a great feat.

How a copper is taught
to enforce our great law
but when they slip him the
money
he learns to ignore.

When seven astronauts die
coloured stories fill the 'Age'
but when hundreds die in
India
there's not even half a page.

Tell me why on my reports
I rate a high B,
but my inner self happiness,
only marks an E.

God, please tell me the
answers,
please tell them right now,
tell me them in full
tell me why, when and how.

When you give your
explanations
the answers better fit;
and you'd better speak fast
'cos the trains about to hit.

R.I.P.

Year 11 student
An Australian secondary
school

8

Where To From Here?

Things haven't been getting any easier for kids in the past few years!

I'm not making excuses for the strange things teenagers often do. I'm not saying that music or any other influence taken on its own is the total cause of a young person's depression or anxiety. Taken together, though, the influences described in the foregoing chapters contribute to the world young people live in—their subculture, their particular window on the universe. Unless their parents, leaders and friends empathise with the world of the young, they can never hope to offer real reassurance and guidance to the young people they care about.

The first section of this book is about problems. The second is devoted to answers; simple principles which we can all apply in one way or another, in practical settings, to bring about positive changes in the hearts and hopes of the young persons we care about. I will try to avoid 'quick fix' suggestions because, when dealing with the complexities of human nature, there are none that work. However, one should never mistake that which sounds simple for that which is simplistic.

I cannot offer a long list of 'One Hundred Things You Should Do If You're Going To Be Parent, Friend Or Youth Worker Of The Year.' My own children are still quite young, so I don't consider myself an expert on parenting and, even as a youth communicator and leader, I've found that the longer you work with the young, the more you discover how little you really know about them!

I have, however, spent thousands of hours counselling, talking to and teaching teenagers. I have the advantage of hearing young people on their own 'turf' —in schools, concerts, restaurants and the like. I have heard them express cries which their parents or adult friends might not have heard or understood.

Prevention of a problem is always better than cure. If we can understand the pressures young people are under, we may be able to reduce the negative effect they could have on the kids we care about. The answer to this nation's youth depression and suicide problem, is not in throwing more money at the thing, as some governments are prone to do. Long-term solutions stem from trying to address the fundamental problems relating to how young people feel about themselves and the world around them, and how capable they feel in managing their lives and planning their futures.

To positively influence these attitudes and perceptions in the minds of the young, we must start by influencing the people who instruct them in life. In the following pages, I will discuss eight statements which I think every teenager would like to make to their parents or other guardians and their teachers, youth pastors, community workers and friends. Chances are, you've heard some of them before, but perhaps it has not occurred to you that they might be more than just casual remarks or empty, cynical gripes. Each one contains a cry for help and understanding. Each represents a need which you and I can help to fill.

Whatever your role in their lives, if you are involved with young people and you care about them, you are important to them. You may be a parent, youth leader or concerned friend. It is my sincere hope that, as you read, you will come upon one o r two ideas which might relate to where you and your young friends are at right now. I pray that you will seek God's help in applying these practical principles to their needs.

Young people need us!

9

How Much Does Your Love Cost?

The Need For Personal Value

Every teenage person wants above all else to be loved, and loved unconditionally.

On hundreds of occasions during my years of work among young people, I have looked a teenager in the eye and boldly told them, 'You are not an accident of birth.' I've seen so many kids just break when they've heard those simple words! Why do those words have such a powerful impact? Perhaps it's because so many teenagers and young adults have either been told, or lead to believe, that they are not wanted or accepted by those who matter the most to them.

Some years ago psychologist Charles Cooley gave us an important concept, to which I alluded in chapter five, which he called the 'Looking Glass Self'. Cooley suggested that early in our lives we begin to form pictures of who we are. These images are based on what other people—especially people who are important to us— seem to think of us. In other words, if my father, mother, school teacher or some other important person in my early life continually tells me, with their words or actions, that I am an idiot, clumsy or ugly, then that is what I will come to believe about myself. That is how I will come to behave.

Making An Impression

From early childhood we human beings form images of ourselves based on signals given to us by others. Every one of these images is stored somewhere on the surface of the brain.

In the I950s there was very little in the way of medical help available to people who suffered from epilepsy. Medications which now help epileptics lead full and normal lives were not developed at that time. One man who was doing something to reduce their suffering was a doctor by the name of Penfield. He developed an operation which could help alleviate the effects of epilepsy in the more severe cases. By making small cuts on the surface of a person's brain, he could sometimes reduce or even halt the 'electrical storms' which caused epileptic fits.

For safety reasons, however, the operation had to be performed while the patient was still conscious! Only a local anaesthetic could be used. The surgeon removed a small piece of the skull and then proceeded to make the cuts before replacing the section of skull and sewing up the skin. It does sound gruesome, but it offered relief to suffering people.

Interestingly, the doctor found that, as he made contact with the surface of the brain using a tiny probe, the patients would often experience very vivid recollections of events in their past. For example, grown adults would recollect details of childhood birthday parties. When the probe was moved to another point the same person, still wide awake, would recall something completely different from another period of his or her life. These recollections were not hallucinatory but vivid memories of actual sensory experiences, such as the sights, sounds and even smells associated with even mundane events.

The brain stores absolutely everything we have ever experienced no matter how seeming trivial. Everything parents tell their children about themselves is stockpiled somewhere in the mind's computer and, if the same image is fed in enough times, it will invariably affect their behaviour at some point in their lives.

Psychologists have given us another clue as to the power of our words and actions in shaping the minds and attitudes of young friends. The concept is called anchoring and it refers to the way in which words become even more powerful when reinforced by other strong non-verbal signals. If you repeatedly tell a three-year-old child that he or she is a pest, you are sending strong messages about the child's self-worth. When you combine that verbal message with non-verbal reinforcement—when, for example, you raise or shake your fist and grit your teeth as you say it—the words are given greater gravity in the child's mind. After all, you are three times his or her size and you are important. The child relies upon you for information about the way the world is.

Growing Pains
Parents, from their very earliest years our children pick up messages about their personal worth from us, just as we did from our parents. There are, though, other people who also have a profound influence upon the young, including other family members, relatives, friends, teachers and the heroes of popular youth culture.

As children grow into adolescence, they add to the clues parents have provided as to their identity those which come from their peers and culture. I have found that one of the most potent messages young people are receiving from the culture around them, if not first from their parents, is that worth and value are based upon either looks or performance.

You only have to make a very cursory study of the TV sitcoms made for the youth market to see what I mean. TV is all about appearances. When did you last see one of the young stars of these shows who had a problem with a bad case of acne? Or an abrasive, awkward personality? The 'average' teenage star lives behind a far from average image. In TV sitcom-land, life's difficulties arrive and then depart all within a very tidy half-hour format! Sitcom stars live in a fantasy world, far removed from real teenage life.

The world in which the teenager lives is a world which places inordinate value on appearances. Adolescence is a period in an individual's life when he or she feels decidedly awkward, to say the least, about the way he or she looks. Our bodies change rapidly during this time and we have to come to grips with a whole new physiology. This apprehensiveness is not helped by the fact that, at this same point in our lives, we are beginning to look for an identity outside of the home environment and our parents' influence, among people of our own age, who are themselves fairly insecure people. Peer groups can do a real 'demolition job' on kids who don't look good.

Bill Cosby has said that puberty was the time when he discovered that 'God has a sense of humour.' It was the time when he most wanted to impress girls and yet the time when he also got pimples and his voice broke.

Another idea young people are prone to imbibe from their culture is that an individual's value is largely based on how he or she performs, or what he or she achieves. Many people in our society today appear to be obsessed with the notion of being 'number one.' Nobody wants to be second in line; success is equated with being the best and nothing but the best. Our worship of this kind of success has placed enormous pressure on young people. They often feel torn between the pressure to conform to their peer group's expectations and, at the same time, to satisfy the aspirations of their parents and society at large.

A popular pastor friend of mine relates the story of a teenage girl who, because she didn't think her life was interesting enough to attract the kind of respect and attention she wanted from her friends, concocted a whole new personal history for herself. She made up a story about a past drug problem, alcohol addiction and a few other 'niceties' which she felt would help consolidate her existence in her social set.

The Bear Necessities

I started my life of public speaking when I was around five or six years of age. It was a very inauspiscious beginning. I had to round up my own audience, which consisted of a horde of family teddy bears and my brother, Ian, who was unfortunate enough to be four years my junior and quite unable to refuse.

I owe a lot to those bears. I had this one favourite. By the time I was three years of age, he'd been everywhere with me. We'd been in and out of some real scraps together and he was looking just a little tired and ragged around the edges. His hair was falling out in clumps and his clothing was looking decidedly pre-worn (very trendy now). He looked like he was having a teddy bear mid-life crisis.

Now, as you will appreciate, little kids are not stupid! They might talk like R2 D2, but they seem to have their hand on everything that goes down around them (I personally think they're secretly taking notes on us for God to use on judgement day!). I knew exactly what happened to that favourite bear of mine each time I left the room. I'd sit him in the largest armchair I could find so that he'd be comfortable while I was out. On my return, I'd invariably find him face down on the floor, 'eating carpet', while some huge (they all looked huge to me then) adult-type person occupied that chair.

That bear didn't get a whole lot of respect when I was out. But when I returned, you'd better believe things changed for the better. When I was around, that little hunk of shagpile got some love and concern from even the biggest, most hardened adult. That toy—who looked for all the world like he'd prefer to believe in toy euthanasia—had value in my house just because I loved it.

I often tell that story to young people to illustrate the importance of knowing that God loves us. We may not look like much to anyone else, but, because God loves us, we have value on his earth.

Romans 12:2 is a powerful part of the Bible. Listen to this: 'Don't copy the behaviour and customs of this world, but be a new and different person with a fresh newness in all you do and think.' God has warned against having our value system determined by the thinking of the secular world around us. The Christian ethic and value system is often vastly different from that espoused by our secular world. Having been exposed for so much of their daily lives to unfair and ungodly measures of self-worth, young people will often need to be reassured in three areas.

The young people we care for need to know that our love for them is based on a firm and unchanging decision we have made—that our love is an act of will not of whim. We have decided that, no matter how irresponsible, impertinent or careless they may be at times, they will still have value for someone in this world. We have decided that, because God values them, because in His eyes they are not an accident (He doesn't have accidents even if you and I do!) but an important planned event, we will give them the benefit of the doubt, even when they appear at their most unlovely.

Secondly, they need to know that true success is not being the best at everything. In fact, a successful person may not ever be the world's best at anything! Chances are, no matter how hard we try and how well we do a thing, someone somewhere out there in the wide world will do it better!

Thirdly, young people need to know that success is not doing something—anything—perfectly the first time they try it. (They may never do it perfectly). A thing worth doing is worth messing up a couple of times before you do it well. Adopting a value system which promotes perfect performance can have tragic consequences for the young. (See chapter seven).

How Much Does Your Love Cost?

Like all human beings, teenagers crave to be accepted for who they are, not for what they can do, or for their looks. These are systems of value judgement which Jesus told us to avoid. He said that love is first a commitment—a pledge to do what is best for the other, despite one's feelings toward them at times. He taught that, 'Whoever desires to save his life [looking after "number one"], will lose it; but whoever loses his life lays it down] for my sake and the sake of the gospel [in the service of others] will find his life' (Mark 8:35, brackets mine).

Young people are often led to believe that, in order to be truly fulfilled in life, the first and most important thing for them to do is to 'find out who they really are'. One way they do this is by experimenting in sexual relationships. Once you've slept with a few people and discovered what you like in a partner, they're told, then you may be ready to commit yourself to one lasting relationship. Jesus' words outline a radically different path to happiness. For Jesus, commitment comes first and 'finding yourself' follows, as a result of decisive commitment. We teach teenagers this priority in the way we commit ourselves to them and their best interests.

Dear parent, how long is it since you told your kids that you love them—no strings attached? Don't assume that they will just have taken it for granted because you've always kept them in food and clothing. Youth worker, how often do you make a practice of reaffirming your love for the young people you are responsible for? Concerned friend, when did you last tell the young person you care about how you feel toward him or her? Go out of your way to tell them. Put an arm around their shoulder and, well, tell them that they have value just as they are, because both you and God love them as they are.

Do it fast.

10
Do You Like Me?

The Need For Identity

There's a lot said and sung about love these days, but a song I heard on the radio a while back made me question just how much this world really knows about the subject. The chorus of this little country rock number, played on a station which targets teenage kids, went along these lines: 'I love you too much to ever start likin' you / So don't ever think we could just be good friends / 'Cause I love you too much to ever start likin' you.'

I love you too much to start liking you? Question: What kind of love is this? Answer: It's not love at all. Yet it adequately sums up how many teenagers today see love. When they hear you say 'I love you', they strain those words through a whole network of messages about love, which they've been receiving from both the real world and the pop-teen culture around them. 'Love' is often thought of as something you do between bedsheets. 'Liking' is an altogether different thing.

Parents, your kids can actually hear you say you love them and still be left wondering whether you also actually like them! And being liked is one thing young people crave more than most parents think.

Some years ago, Janis Ian wrote and made a hit out of a song called Seventeen. It poignantly expresses the way many young people see themselves. Ian's lyrics tell of skin problems and a lack of social graces; of imaginary lovers, loneliness and rejection. One line sums up the whole song: 'It isn't all it seems at seventeen.'

Choosing Teams

In more than one of the public talks I share with teenagers and young adults, I open up with the story of how I disliked physical education class at school. Actually, disliked is too mild a word—I hated it! For two reasons: first of all because we all had to wear shorts for sport. I was a little on the thin side and nicknames such as 'sticks' didn't do much to boost my performance on the field.

The other reason I loathed 'phys. ed.' was the tribal ritual the teachers called 'choosing teams'. Basically this consisted of two macho-man team captains voting publicly on who were the most worthwhile human beings in the school (ie. who could kick a football furthest). Invariably, me and my mates, members of the school chess squad, were left until last in this 'humane' little ritual.

I'll always go on to share some pretty interesting stuff in those public messages, but the thing young people always seem to want to talk to me about afterwards is the 'Choosing Teams' saga. So many of them relate to it: they've experienced the same feelings of inferiority and unpopularity. In one of his excellent books, Dr. James Dobson makes this apt remark: 'What a shame that most teenagers decide they are without human worth when they're between 13 and 15 years of age.'[1]

I've been to some interesting cities in the world and come across some very interesting youth subcultures. There's the punk subculture for example. I think that Dr. Anthony Campolo is correct when he says that the punks actually wear their ugliness on the outside—they dare the world to love them. Their outward appearance reflects their inner feelings about themselves and their world.

There are the 'metal-heads' too. 'Metal' music has long been divided up into many different sub-genres, including thrash and glam-metal. Each genre has its own following, who wear just the right clothes and talk just the right slang to show their allegiance to the group.

The 'gothics' are another intriguing bunch. They wear basic black with heavy eyeshadow and caked-on facial make-up. To them Morticia Addams of TV's *Addams Family* is a fashion queen.

Chances are, if you were to spy a punk, a metal-head and a gothic walking down the street together, you would say to yourself (among other things): 'These people have absolutely nothing in common!' You would be very wrong. They do in fact share one very important characteristic—they are all conformists. They are trying desperately, each in their own way, to fit in with the crowd, to blend in with their chosen environment.

I have a theory. It says few 'metal' fans listen to their music simply because they enjoy it. The music is more than an auditory experience. It is a badge of membership in their fraternity—listening is a sign that they belong. Many of today's most loyal metal-heads will, in a few years, have stopped listening to metal and will have found other ways to gain acceptance with a new crowd.

Whatever our age we all like to conform, just so that

we don't stand out for all the wrong reasons. As mentioned previously, psychiatrists have told us that most people have two great fears: that they will not be loved and that they will not be able to love in return. The teenager feels the possibility of rejection very keenly indeed.

This is the first of two major reasons I see for the ultra-conformity of many teenagers. Did you know that, in some surveys conducted among western young people, one of the things youth say they are most afraid of is public speaking?

You come to expect answers such as 'nuclear warfare', 'family break-up' and the like, but public speaking? Is that really so dreadful? To a teenager it may very well be front page news right now! Human beings tend to hide all kinds of unpleasant things about themselves under masks of self assurance and nonchalance. A great deal of nervous apprehension is hidden beneath human bravado.

Speaking in public means getting out in front of people and opening yourself to scrutiny. You are the centre of attention, but that is not all it's cracked up to be. You take the risk of failing, falling flat on your face. Public speaking is a frightening prospect for many an adult. For teenagers it can be a nightmare.

The second reason many young people conform has to do with the fact that, for the first time in their lives they are trying to establish their identities in the context of the world at large. As small children they were content to believe only what their parents and close family members told them about who they were. Now that they've caught a glimpse of a larger scene beyond the letterbox, they want greater reassurance of their worth to the world. Hence, they will adopt traits which are foreign

140

to their home environment in order to fit into the 'bigger picture'.

Ego Is Not A Dirty Word

Many people, including Christian people, are afraid of the idea of self-esteem. They confuse building a sound and accurate sense of self with inspiring undesirable pride and arrogance. Self-appreciation is not the equivalent of self-centredness! Self-interest is not another way of saying selfishness.

In fact, self-interest is vital to human survival and success. It is because of self-interest that you seek a certain type of employment, that you marry a particular person, that you indulge in certain enjoyable hobbies. If you are a Christian, you should know that it was partly self-interest which brought you to God. You came to him because you wanted the kind of life He promised you—'life to the full'(John 10:10).

I suppose it could be said that there are two sides to our ego—our sense of who we are. The first we might call personality, the second, pride. When you try to stifle your own or someone else's personality you can produce some horrendous results. We need to help young people grow into a proper appreciation of their own personality while at the same time helping to steer them away from arrogance and self-centred behaviour.

I've met some great young people, each of whom have displayed a fantastic sense of humour. I love anyone who knows how to laugh and how to make me laugh. Yet these same individuals are often the ones who carry the worst insecurities—insecurities partly derived from the fact that their parents or leaders have tried to stifle their natural personality. The role of parents and friends is to help young people channel their natural wit, not to strangle it. The Bible actually commands us to work at the development of positive, balanced self-image. Think on these words from St. Paul in Romans 12:3: 'Don't cherish exaggerated ideas of yourself or your importance, but try to have a sane estimate of your capabilities by the light of the faith that God has given to you all.'

There are two mistakes we can make then. One is exaggerating our own importance in this world; the other is denying that we have anything to offer at all. For a Christian a whole new kind of self-esteem is possible, based not upon human arrogance but on faith in God's nature. I can hold my head high, with dignity and a sense of worth even when the heat is really on, because I know that, whatever my numerous flaws, I have a Father in heaven who sees me as a product of His revitalising love and power!

Do I Count?

Young people must possess the three major elements of a healthy self-esteem. The first is the feeling that they belong, that they 'fit in' somewhere—in the home, the community, the school, the office, factory or the church.

In his book, *Healing the Masculine Soul,* writer and teacher Gordon Dalbey relates with conviction the affect a visit to his grandfather's home had on his life and work. As a mature adult of 42 years of age, Dalbey had come to a point of discouragement in relation to his ministry, which seemed to be going nowhere fast. At a time in mid-life when self-doubt and agonising questions about his career path filled his mind, he was offered the opportunity to see the place where his father had grown up.

He tells of seeing the family home for the first time—a small millworker's house, little more than a car length wide. He tells of the old smokestacks which were once a part of the steelworks where his grandfather toiled for sixty hours a week beside the blazing furnace. His grandfather had died of cancer at the age of 54, with 'virtually no pension to show for his work.' What affect did this pilgrimage have on a highly educated modern man, disillusioned with life and uncertain about his future?

'As I boarded my return flight to California later that week,' says Dalbey, 'I knew I would never be the same. I had come to that place a world traveller, rootless, unfocused, even careless with my life, as if I had been cast out into the world from no real place and with no real identity or lasting purpose.

'I returned a son—a man who comes from a place, from specific men, and who is responsible to make the most of his own role in history as they did in theirs.'[2]

This account graphically illustrates the value of a sense of belonging, of knowing you come from some-where. If it can have this effect on a middle-aged man, what good might it do for a teenager? How can a young person, any person, know where they are headed if they can't tell where they started—not just geographically, but emotionally? If there are no strong ties to the past, through relationships with people who are important to us, how can the future appear promising and secure?

The benefits of a healthy extended family cannot be overestimated. I know that in my own experience I have benefitted greatly from knowing my many aunts, uncles, cousins and my grandparents. I enjoyed a sense of belonging from early days and it carried me through many a tough decision as a teenager. I draw great strength from it even now. It is not possible, of course, to manufacture that kind of family relationship where it does not exist. Many parents have become estranged either emotionally or geographically from their own parents and siblings. Parents, can, however, ensure that teenagers enjoy some network of stable, positive relationships with other adults beyond the home. They can give their teenagers a sense of roots, without taking them back to the place where the family tree was planted.

For example, parents, if your teenagers are not part of a good church which has a well-rounded family programme and caters for young peoples' special needs, encourage them into one as soon as you can. The church of Jesus Christ is not just another alternative social club. Good local churches recognise that they are families of God's people. Your teenager can derive a great sense of belonging from involvement with a group of committed Christians. If you're not a part of a church like that, set the example. Don't just send your kids, take them.

I recall on one or two occasions, when I was a youth pastor, having a parent from outside the church ring to express their concern at how their teenage child was changing as a result of our involvement with him or her. The parent wanted to know what we were 'doing to' his son or daughter.

'Look,' they would say, 'my boy used to be just like his mates (ie. drinking, smoking pot and generally going nowhere fast!) but now that he's going to church, he doesn't want to do those things anymore. What's wrong with him?'

I could never understand why some parents felt happier when their children were up to no good, or slowly killing themselves, than when they started to spend time around positive people who helped them get their lives straight.

144

The second aspect of a healthy self-image, which every young person needs, is the feeling of being capable. I recall hearing the Duke of Edinburgh state in an interview that he had always tried to instil in his children the knowledge that they were good at something. It didn't matter if their talents seemed few, because as they began to feel good about their prowess in one activity, some of the confidence they derived from it would gradually find its way into other areas of life. A very sound theory, I say.

Thirdly, there is the feeling of worth. This is so important to young people and we touched on it earlier. Every time you assign a negative nickname to a teenager, you are helping to destroy his or her sense of worthiness. Teenage people want so very much to be 'normal'. Any personal trait you emphasise with names such as 'fat face', 'big ears', 'big mouth', 'fatso', 'four eyes', 'skinny' and the like, will immediately take on greatly exaggerated proportions in the mind of a young person.

I don't know why we expect young people to think this kind of thing is all in fun. What's funny about having your flaws plastered all over town? Today's youth desperately want to know that they are liked.

Building Self Esteem

1. Spend Time

When was the last time you showed your young friends that you actually enjoy their company, that you just like being with them? Someone has said that if you're wondering what to spend on a young person, spend time! Another writer made the statement that, 'the word love is spelt T.I.M.E.' When did your young friend last enjoy the pleasure of uninterrupted time with you, doing things he or she enjoys?

2. Show Respect

When did you last show teenage friends that you respect them and their opinions on a matter, that you don't dismiss what they say out of hand? When did you last actually ask their opinion on a decision you are making, or on some world event? When did they last hear you apologise or seek their forgiveness for something you did, simply because their feelings are important to you?

Teenagers, unlike small children, have the capacity to recognise that they deserve a certain degree of respect just for what they are. This helps to explain the defensiveness of some teenagers. Teens can be defensive when they feel that their sensitive ego is under attack and that they are likely to lose ground in the eyes of those whose respect they crave.

3. Use The Power Of Touch

Parents, do your kids know that you feel good about them? Have you touched your teenage kids recently?

In our society, the power of touch is a much underrated one. We speak of someone having 'the magic touch', 'a human touch', or being a 'soft touch'. We talk about people being 'touchy', 'thin-skinned', 'thick-skinned' or 'clingy'. We say that we 'lose touch', 'get the feel' for something, 'grapple' with problems and have a 'firm grip' on things. We testify to the importance of touch by the amount of popular vocabulary we devote to it. Yet we seem so afraid of actually touching other people.

The human body is built for touch. The largest organ in

the body is the skin. It does more than simply hold our insides in! It actually collects and conveys important messages to our brain—messages about our environment and our relationship to it.

Some psychologists, such as the behaviourist John Broadus Watson, have argued that children are to be raised in a very mechanical way, with as little attention as possible given to sentimentality, touch and intimacy. The small child must not be spoiled with affection. Said Watson: 'There is a sensible way of treating children . . . never hug or kiss them, never let them sit on your lap. If you must, kiss them once on the forehead when you say goodnight. Shake hands with them in the morning. Give them a pat on the head if they have made an extraordinarily good job of a difficult task.'[3]

That approach may sound very uncomplicated and sophisticated, but it is in fact very cruel. This kind of detachment can produce sad results. One callgirl, when asked why she had taken to prostitution, replied: 'In a way, I used sex to be held.' One authority, reporting on 20 women who had three or more illegitimate pregnancies, said: 'Eight of the 20 reported that they were consciously aware that sexual activity, for them, was the price to be paid for being cuddled and held.'[4] For some people, sex is to be tolerated in order to gain touch. Lack of meaningful touch starts some people on the road to promiscuous living.

It would not be stretching things too far to suggest that there might be a link between the current epidemic in teen pregnancies and the need in young people for physical affection. Ann Landers, a US newspaper journalist whose regular column is read by 70 million people, asked her female readers to submit an answer to the following question on sexual intimacy: 'Would you be

147

content to be held close and treated tenderly and forget about "the act" [of intercourse]?' Of the 100,000 replies she received, 72% said 'Yes'. Of those, 40% were under 40 years of age.[5]

Touch deprivation has also been linked with excessive masturbation in some young people. 'The relationship between tactile deprivation in infancy and childhood and sex is clearly evident in the many reported cases of early excessive masturbation in children. In the absence or withdrawal of warm tactile stimulation, the child sometimes turns to his own body for gratification.'[6]

Dr. James H. Prescott from the National Institute of Child Health and Human Development in the US also sees a link between lack of touch and violent behaviour patterns. 'Deprivation of physical pleasure,' he states, 'is a major ingredient in the expression of physical violence.' He has found that the presence of physical pleasure inhibits the presence of violence.[7]

Homosexual behaviour patterns can also at times be traced to a lack of meaningful closeness between a child and its parents, in particular the parent of the same sex. Gordon Dalbey quotes the director of a Christian ministry to homosexuals in California as saying that a child needs 'affirming relationships with the same sex, especially the same-sex parent' in order to gain 'self-worth and clear sense of gender.' In the majority of cases, says this Christian leader, his clients 'attest to the fact that gay sex wasn't really the motivating factor in their homosexual pursuits, while same-sex intimacy was.'[8] In their case, the need was emotional rather than erotic.

Giving a teenager a hug, or a pat on the back, a handshake or a reassuring arm around the shoulder can convey a powerful message of acceptance.

4. Express Trust

Does your teenage child or friend know that you trust them? In practical terms, your level of trust needs to be a realistic one, based upon the individual's age and experience. Be honest about your level of trust. Parent, if, because you know human nature all too well, you don't trust things to go smoothly when your 16-year-old daughter starts staying out past 11 pm, tell her the truth. Trust is not given willy-nilly. It is accorded in proportion to self-responsibility and that grows with maturity.

5. Be Secure

Let me leave one more thought with you here. Paranoia in parents only ever produces frustration and perplexity in teenagers. After all, no matter how bad the stats read in the local papers, not every kid is on drugs or 'sleeps around.' You must treat each young person according to his or her own merits and your level of trust must be seen to grow as the individual does.

11

Elvis is Dead

The Need For Empathy

'In my day, you wouldn't have got away with that, young lady.'

'Who cares what you were allowed to do? We're living in the '90s. Things have changed, you know.'

Parent, youth worker, how many times have you been through a conversation like that one? If you're like many of the parents of teenagers I know, you've rehearsed it over and over with your kids until it's repeated almost verbatim whenever a difference of opinion arises!

As annoying as it may seem to you, there is a certain amount of bald truth in what that young person is telling you. Things have changed a lot since you were their age. Sure, people have remained, at the very core of human nature, much the same. People today feel the same pain, fear the same rejection and face the same questions about the meaning of human existence as previous generations. Yet, as the first half of this book demonstrates, young people now face at an early age issues and questions which, if you had a fairly average upbringing, you did not deal with until you were a good deal older, if at all.

There are five little words which never fail to kill a conversation with a teenager. What are they? 'When I was your age . . .' Dropping this line into a conversation with a teenager can produce the same effect as lighting a match in a fireworks factory. Perhaps that's because using phrases such as this one demonstrates that no attempt is being made to understand the world these young people are living in.

The Bible gives us much helpful practical information on how to make relationships work. Romans 12:15 gives us some valuable advice: 'When others are happy be happy with them. If they are sad, share in their sorrow.' This is what we now call being empathic. One of the greatest ways you can demonstrate love for someone is by showing them that you are trying to understand their problem, to see their circumstances as they do, to be involved in their situation.

There are times when teenagers do things which even they don't understand (and you thought it was just antiquated you getting out of touch!) Sometimes, especially in matters of the heart, teenagers can seem unpredictable, even incomprehensible, to adults. When they talk of having 'fallen in love', you can't help feeling that they might just as quickly fall out of it again at any moment and for no apparent reason. Adolescent people do tend to wear their hearts on their sleeves. Sadly, as we grow older we tend to discard some of that honesty about ourselves, burying it under masks and images we have picked up to protect ourselves from rejection.

Teenagers can be, well, just more honest about their feelings than adults are, but they sometimes lack the ability of mature adults to balance feelings with wisdom, commitment and forethought. We should not stifle their refreshing honesty, even if it does look like just plain fickleness at times. Instead, we need to build onto it all the stabilising qualities that will help them keep a grip on the passions and whims of youth.

In order to gain the respect and trust of young people, I must demonstrate a desire to get involved with them, in their struggles and their challenges. When I seek to become actively involved in someone else's life, I show them that their experience has value for me, that they are important to me. Once I have gained their respect, I will be able to influence young people for the good.

Wearing The Other Guy's Reeboks

If this book does; nothing else for you, I hope it will help you to empathise with the youth of today, to 'get into their shoes' for a while and see their world and its pressures as they do. It's not so important that you actually understand perfectly how kids think. It's whether you try to empathise that counts. Empathy involves a series of simple disciplines:

Listen Attentively: One of the most satisfying things in life must be having someone else listen to your 'story', your account of your life or part of it, past or present. Young people enjoy this as much as anybody. It is vital that you give your undivided attention. Sometimes, when other matters are pressing on you, you'd be best to set an appointed time for a discussion, to be sure that you can afford that kind of attentiveness.

Give Feedback On What You Hear. As you listen, repeat, in your own words, what you understand your teenage child or friend to be telling you. It's essential that you do express what you're hearing in your own terms, as this shows you are really trying to come to grips with what the young person is feeling. It also provides opportunity for them to correct any misconceptions you may have.

Identify Content And Feelings In What You Hear. It's not just what your young friend is going through, but how they are feeling about it, which is important to them. Do your best to give feedback which deals not just with information but with the emotions they are expressing (eg. 'You feel cheated about that, don't you?'; 'I can hear a lot of anger in what you're telling me. Are you very angry?').

Remember: What really counts is not how you see the situation or the problem but how it appears to the person you are seeking to help. A matter which seems trivial to you may be of enormous importance to younger, less experienced people. Treat the information you are given with respect and, where required, with confidentiality.

If you are a parent or youth worker, and you are wise, you will realise this—one of the most important things which can come out of the painful times young people experience, is the knowledge that you are their friend, that you will stand by them, come what may. When their whole universe is turned unceremoniously on its ear one week, only to be painfully rearranged again a week later, they want to know that someone out there will function as a steadfast anchor for them. Someone who sometimes understands them better than they do themselves. Someone who will cheer them on from the sidelines, even when the game they're playing feels out of their control.

My Kid The Head Banger!
This brings to mind one occasion when I was lecturing a

group of adult college students on the importance of empathising with the young. I gave certain practical ideas on how a parent or youth worker might better come to understand the world teenagers live in. Instead of turning the kids' music down, for example, I suggested sitting down and actually listening to it—especially the lyrics.

At the end of the course I asked the students to share on any aspect of the programme which had particularly challenged or helped them. One woman stood to her feet and, quietly and uncertainly at first, began to recount her reaction to some of my ideas. Her first reaction had been one of anger. How could I suggest she listen to the very music which she knew was having such a destructive influence on her son? Having spent so many hours in the past taking him to task over his particular brand of 'metal', this might be seen by him as an admission of defeat or even tacit approval.

Anyway, she had enough courage to give my suggestion a try. One evening as he sat in his bedroom with his headphones on, she asked if she might be able to listen to the music with him. She almost had to pick him up from the floor! He wired up another set of 'cans' and they sat there on the floor listening to the pounding sounds together (at slightly less than normal volume). Now, almost in tears as she described his reaction to our class, this concerned mother told us that what followed was the most positive and open discussion she and her son had enjoyed in years. She spoke her mind on his music, but now she was able to speak out of something other than ignorance. Her son responded to her attempt to understand him better, even if he did not yet see the problem with the music.

I felt proud of this mother who, at some risk to her

own stand on an important issue, had really started to come to grips with the way her teenage son saw the world.

Many young people suffer terribly from feelings of isolation and alienation from their families and leaders. They have a strong desire to share their problems with others, but feel unable to do so. Some cover their pain by seeking refuge in their peer groups, where they feel they are understood. Some seek solace in a bottle, or with a syringe. Others simply withdraw from everyone. All the while, their parents, family members and friends want to help. Where does helping start? With a willingness to listen. With a commitment to practice the principles of empathy.

12

Don't Treat Me Like A Child!

The Art Of Discipline

There is probably no area in which conflict between parents and youth workers and maturing young people is as guaranteed as in that of discipline. Most teenagers will not disagree that sound discipline is, at least in the long term, a beneficial thing. Conflict arises on the matter of just what is fair and healthy discipline right now.

The Bible has long been a resource on the subject of sound discipline. It states clearly that parental discipline is an integral part of love in the home. In recent times, many parents have become afraid that applying traditional forms of discipline might harm their child's delicate psyche.

In 1945 Dr. Benjamin Spock released a book entitled *Baby And Child Care*. It sold more than 28 million copies. Spock's ideas on disciplining children centred on allowing the child to do pretty much his or her own thing. He discouraged spanking and taught that simple reasoning with a child would produce better results.

Later, Spock made this observation: 'The greatest problem with parents today is their inability to be firm . . . Nowadays there are more parents who are afraid of their children than children who are afraid of their parents. And this is the first time in the history of the human race that this has ever happened. Submissiveness only encourages children to be more difficult and makes the parents more resentful, until they explode in anger."

Discipline: Who Needs The Aggravation?

It is, of course, true that the parents' or youth workers' role in discipline can be overdone, as it has been in not a few cases. Discipline which is underdone also produces sad fruit in the life of a young person. Youth who have never been properly disciplined grow up without the security of clear guidelines for acceptable behaviour, and suffer socially and emotionally as a result.

Discipline can only be undertaken fairly when the person administering it understands its proper basic aims. It seems to me that there are basically three stages in the development of a child from its very early days to adulthood. Think back upon your own development.

In the beginning, there was dependence. You were completely reliant on the goodwill and tender loving care of your parents for every single thing that was good for you. You could not dress yourself, feed yourself or attend to your own toilet activity. Your fate was in the lap of the big people out there.

Dependence was followed by what you thought was independence. Parents, this is where your teenagers sometimes think they are right now. Do you remember saying (or at least wanting to say) to your parents such things as: 'Don't tell me what to do with my life . . . I don't need your help . . . It's my life and I'll live it how I want to . . .'? This was a time for checking out your limits, for experimenting with the sense of self-determination you were beginning to experience.

You will probably remember moments when you discovered that, though you would like to live more or less as a law unto yourself, you could not do so without being a very lonely and unpopular person. Other people did have certain expectations of you. Even your compatriots in teenagedom made certain rules which you were expected to obey. You were expected to behave in certain ways, and to play certain roles in society with others.

The ability to make your own choices in life, but to do so in a way that demonstrates a sense of responsibility for your fellow man, is what real maturity is all about. Adulthood is about something beyond both helpless dependence and arrogant independence, it is about interdependence. Interdependence says, to other human beings, 'I may not need you for everything I will ever do, but I cannot live without you. I need you for the important things in life—fellowship, relationship and fulfilling my potential.'

Dear embattled parent and youth worker, your teenage friends are doing a whole lot of adjusting right now. They are trying to make up the ground between the first two stages of life and come safely through to the third. The discipline they need, is not so much punishment as it is the establishing of guidelines for living. Those guidelines will provide a foundation for the development of their own decision making faculties.

Young people need to be shown that, with increased freedom to make choices, comes a greater responsibility for the outcome of those decisions. Contrary to what seems to be popular belief these days, while human beings are free to make choices they are not free to escape the consequences of bad decisions. The purpose of discipline is to lead youth to appreciate responsibility.

This is why, as a teenager grows, you will need to carefully think through, and adjust, the standards you are imposing on him or her. You need to have reasons for wanting them to live by certain rules. The natural human response to any new directive is: 'What's in it for me?' I know, it's not one of our more noble instincts, but it is there. If you are able to explain how their lives will benefit from a particular rule, it may make it easier for teenagers to comply, without losing face in the process. In my discussions with thousands of young people and their parents, I have been able to make observations about the subject of discipline and what it requires of the parents. I submit the following thoughts for the benefit of both parents and concerned youth workers. They may help you to steer your way through the maze of possibilities in this minefield called discipline.

1. Discipline Is Risky Business!

It seems to me that disciplining teenagers means taking a risk—the risk that they may misunderstand, resent or become angry with you. I experienced this feeling in my work both as a youth pastor and later as senior pastor of a local church. Young people do not always give you the 'Most Appreciated Person In My Life' award for taking the trouble to discipline them.

Nevertheless, you can be sure that youth need you to take that risk, no matter how painful it seems—for you or for them. I look back now, at my years as youth pastor in a fairly large church, and note that some of the young people who presented me with the biggest problems, and whom I had to discipline the most, have turned out to be the most committed to me personally. Now adults, a couple of them still write every so often just to keep in touch. I still take a keen interest in their lives, because I was able to make an investment in them. The more you invest into someone else, the more you want them to do well.

Some parents and youth workers are simply too afraid, or too apathetic, to apply a standard for behaviour. Failing to do this is like building a Formula One racing car and forgetting to install brakes. Discipline teaches kids acceptable limits and sets them up for 'safe driving' in society.

2. Discipline Requires Instruction

All too often, we adults expect teenagers to know what it is we want from them, without our ever having to tell them. We assume that they're already thinking on our wavelength and, when they fail to do what is expected, we react in anger. Many kids, who really want to please their parents, are frustrated with the rules at home, because the rules aren't clear.

It has long been accepted in the field of teaching motivational skills that people always perform better if they are told exactly what good performance will look like. An employer, for example, needs to clearly show his employees what he expects of them, breaking his goals down into measurable, practical and realistic tasks. Discipline in the home, youth group or church needs the same approach.

In just three years, Jesus managed to shape a group of fishermen, tax collectors and the like, into a history making, revolutionary outfit. When Jesus taught His followers, He didn't simply give them a few pat answers to life's questions and send them out to fend for themselves. First, He instructed them thoroughly in the practical skills they would need if they were to fulfil His demands. He trained His disciples in practical terms.

They knew what was expected of them. In shaping the lives of young people we would do well to follow His example.

When rules are made, in the home, church, or school, they need to be expressed in as practical terms as possible. For example, telling a teenager, 'You must be home by 10 pm', is much more explicit than 'Be home by a reasonable hour.'

3. Discipline Requires Flexibility

Parents and leaders, whilst you shouldn't back off when it comes to the discipline of teenagers, you should take account of the fact that there will need to be adjustments every so often. The parameters you set for a six-year-old's behaviour are unsuitable for application to a 15-year-old. You can't expect a 17-year-old guy or girl to happily comply with the same level of discipline he or she was used to at 13. The older young people grow, the more frequent the adjustments will need to be.

As a parent or youth leader, you should give teenagers as much freedom as you think they can handle, and be there to give support, advice, encouragement or, where necessary, a rebuke along the way. Also, as your young friends mature, you will need to allow them more and more input into the rule-making process. Your confidence in them will help them develop confidence in themselves.

Of course, unless you possess super-human powers of persuasion, you will sometimes have trouble convincing teenagers that the standards you have set are the most reasonable in the circumstances. Sometimes teenagers use their stinging wit to mock and nag parents, and leaders, into submission. Don't submit!

'Come on, Mum,' they'll confidently say with an I'm-up-with-the-times-and-you're-not smirk, 'Get real for a minute. I know not even **you** could really mean that I have to be in by 10 pm on a Saturday night!'

Don't let them get to you. Stick to your guns when you have to. Some things just won't be negotiable. Remember, poor embattled parent, teacher, or leader, that you do still have the advantage in terms of life experience. Do try and keep your sense of humour, though—it will keep you sane and, to be fair, teenagers do have an ability to laugh at their own foibles (kids have a great capacity for enjoying teen movies which send them up).

4. Discipline Requires Affirmative Action

Some parents and youth workers don't seem able to give teenagers any room to grow. Sticking to old levels of discipline is easiest for them—it doesn't require change —but it leaves young people feeling cocooned and stifled. Others go to the opposite extreme, not knowing where to draw the right line. They allow teenagers to do whatever comes naturally. These young people eventually recognise that they've been cheated out of a valuable resource—the chance to learn to 'fly' for themselves, with the added assurance of an onboard parental safety parachute.

Still others seem to be adept at setting standards and making rules, but hopelessly inadequate at supporting young people as they try to live by those rules. They provide no 'on-the-job' instruction and encouragement and offer no reassurance when kids fail.

An important and often neglected part of disciplining a teenager is just being there. All teenagers want to know that their parents, and the leaders they look up to, will be there to talk things over when they mess up and fall short of the standards which have been set. Supportive, positive discipline of teenagers means dealing in appropriate ways with wrongs done, while showing that you are prepared to anticipate the best from them in the future.

Discipline is treated by many parents and leaders as a punitive thing. They focus on the negative, almost expecting that teenagers will break the rules. Discipline should focus on future positive actions on the part of teenagers, not dwelling on mistakes they have made in the past. For parents, this message is especially important.

Without doubt, one of the saddest parent-child rifts in all history was that which occurred between David, biblical king of Israel, and Absalom, his fugitive son. Following the account of this sorry affair, recorded in 2 Samuel chapters 13 to 18, one cannot help but wonder how the story might have ended had the father been willing to deal more supportively with his children.

The story begins with Absalom killing his older half-brother, Amnon, because he has raped Absalom's sister. Absalom is driven into exile by his father and, when he is eventually allowed to return to Jerusalem, the young man so resents his father that he sets in motion a plan to usurp the throne. David discovers the plot just in time to flee from the city. Later, as the armies of both men fight it out, Absalom is killed in a field, leaving David to grieve a lost son and wonder what might have been.

As you read the sad account, you may feel that certain questions need to be answered in relation to David's fatherhood. Such as: Why is David's house in such an unhappy and fragmented state to begin with? Why does David fail to adequately punish Amnon, leaving the door open for Absalom to become so frustrated with the king's justice that he takes matters into his own hands? Where is the head of the household when Absalom needs to vent his anger and seeks answers to his questions? Where is David after his boy has committed murder? Why does David seem unwilling to sit down and talk things over with Absalom?

With Absalom, David's discipline is punitive. It says, 'The judge's decision is final and no correspondence will be entered into . . . And even if we discussed the situation, it wouldn't change anything. I've lost all confidence in you. You could never change.' As a result, it drives his son further away from him.

David seems to interact with his children only at arm's length. There is no intimacy, no immediacy, in his relationships with either Absalom or Amnon. Family problems are well entrenched before he ever seems to know about them. By then, it is too late to help. There is no support, only rules; no mercy, only law; no discussion, only retribution.

Instead of simply evicting Absalom from the city, David might have tried discussing his side of the story. In that event, Absalom might not have become the usurper that he did. Certainly, we cannot blame the sins of the sons on their father. But, by the time his boys had become men, they had already established patterns of thought and behaviour which David might have been able to change, had he been more closely involved in their development. Perhaps David did not appreciate that being a supportive father would not have detracted from his public image of warrior king and champion of the people.

There is no doubt that David loved Absalom greatly – his heart-rending expression of guilt at the young man's death is evidence of that. How sad, though, that David could only express after two sons were buried what he should have made plain to them while they were alive—

that is, his belief in them, his hopes for them.

Not many modern families face this kind of high drama, but there are many young people today who, like Absalom, resent their parents' discipline because it seems uncaring. I have been a spectator in situations where parents have shown anything but patient commitment to an erring teenager. Nothing can be more soul-destroying for young people than receiving a public tongue-lashing. Nevertheless, I have watched helplessly as parents have berated their kids openly, showing more concern for a rule which has been transgressed than for the transgressor. Their rules were not made to be broken, they say. I say, neither were their children!

The Right Mix

Most parents worry about disipline. Few ever want to find themselves in King David's situation. Sometimes we worry about being too harsh, at other times we fear that we have been too lenient. Despite our fears, there is a balance which can be achieved. We can set and maintain realistic standards, while at the same time allowing room for our youthful charges to grow, and providing them with positive support. We may not achieve the proper mix in every situation—we are human after all. With a little patience, and with God's help, we might succeed in getting close on enough occasions to achieve the desired result, which is responsible living in our kids.

Parents, you may be fairly sure that your teenagers will make some choices which you would have made differently in their position. For example, they may choose a career path you had not foreseen for them. But you have the right to feel you have done well if those decisions are made in a responsible way.

166

13

You Can't Live Your Life Over Again Through Me

The Need To Let Go

I suppose that one of the greatest temptations for all of us in our relationships with young people, is to unwittingly use our involvement with them to deal with our own insecurities and disappointments. If we're not careful, and fail to face up to our frustrations with life, we can find ourselves playing God, and plotting courses for the future of those we love. Parents and leaders, it is as if we think teenagers can live out our own dreams, succeeding where we have failed, atoning for our losses and regrets. Or, because we love them so much, and want to spare them the pain of discovering life for themselves, we meddle unnecessarily in what should be their own journey of discovery.

Some parents, because their upbringing was too liberal and they suffered as a result, seek to impose overly strict codes of behaviour on their children. When their teenager eventually becomes too old to simply be ordered around, the relationship heads off into very rocky waters.

Others react in a similarly extreme way to their own

overly restrictive childhood, by basically giving their kids free rein—permission to do anything they enjoy 'so long as no-one else gets hurt.' Sadly, life is seldom that simple—people do get hurt, not least of all the teenagers themselves, as they are not yet prepared emotionally or psychologically for what their hormones and sense of adventure want them to experience. Before we can assist younger people in discovering who they are, we need to look long and hard at ourselves.

Take Responsibility For Your Own Mistakes

Perhaps the saddest lesson to be learned from working with young people, is the fact that all too often their problems can be traced to their home life, and to their parents' troubles, which originated in even earlier times. So many parents are putting their teenage children through the same hell they went through and once vowed never to inflict upon their offspring.

'When I have kids,' they said, 'I won't treat them like I was treated. I'll give them all the love I didn't have.'

But their kids don't ever receive the promised inheritance. It's like a wheel the family lives in for generations —each new generation will invariably return to the same low point experienced by their ancestors. The cycle can be broken, but there is only one way it can be done. We must take responsibility for our own mistakes and failures.

Late one evening a man rang me for counselling. He had never met me, but had heard of me and found my number in the phone book. He asked if I might be able to help him with a problem he was having. He was a Christian, he said, and wanted to know the proper course of action for his situation. I told him I would try to help and asked him to tell his story.

'I'm married,' he began. 'I have several children and we've been a happy family for years now. I really love my wife and kids; I've tried to do everything I can to provide for their needs. They mean a lot to me.' With a home life like this, I was beginning to wonder what the problem could be.

He went on: 'But you see, well, I also have a secretary. I don't quite know how it happened, but I've fallen in love with her. Please understand, I don't love my wife any less, it's just that I feel like God would really have me go and live with my secretary—you know, so that I can love her as myself, like Jesus said. What do you think I should do?'

I asked him if he, as a professing Christian, was in the habit of reading the Bible. He said that he was. 'What does the Bible say about your situation?' I enquired.

'Well . . . aaar . . . Look, I don't think you really understand. I didn't mean for this to happen, it just did! We worked closely together and, well, there's a chemistry between us. We just fell for each other.'

Unfortunately, there was not much more I could say to that man. How can you help someone who won't take any responsibility for who they are and what they do?

A number of psychiatrists the world over, now agree that people need to be re-taught about personal responsibility for their actions. Their motive for this suggestion is an interesting one. Unless we accept responsibility for our own actions, they claim, we will be people without hope. You see, if I have had nothing to do with getting myself into a problem, neither will I be able to do anything to get out of it. Hope comes when I accept that my actions do count, they do have an effect, for good or ill.

We need to admit to our own failures, not so that we drag ourselves down into the mire of despair, but so that we may rid ourselves of counter-productive escapism, and begin finding ways to build on those weaknesses.

Admit And Deal With Your Own Anger

We must also face up to our resentments and hidden anger. Bitterness is basically allowing the past to rule the present and dictate to the future. Think about it: If I'm harbouring bitterness against someone I carry that bitterness with me into every new relationship I form. The one event I'd rather forget is carried with me every day through bitter thoughts.

Life is not a videotape. We cannot simply wind it back to the point in time where we were hurt, erase that section, then fast forward to the now. The fact is we all do get hurt. And this is not the way God intended it to be. As Francis Schaeffer has said, 'In the midst of a fallen world things are abnormal; they have been changed from that which God had made them originally.'[1] God is touched by our pains, He is not a dispassionate being. When Jesus arrived at the tomb of Lazarus, He wept, not just for His fallen friend, but for all mankind. When He looked into that tomb He saw all of the suffering, anguish and heartache which characterises human life, all of which eventually culminates in death and He wept for us (John 11). God is moved by our traumas.

There are those who want to know why, if God is such a compassionate person, He lets things go on as they are. Schaeffer again: 'One cannot have the Christian answer that men are really significant in history and then expect God to eradicate every wrong result from that significance while allowing the good aspects of that significance still to operate. If man can influence history, he can influence it for evil and cruelty, as well as for good and noncruelty.'[2]

If God cares at all, some say, how do we explain an

Auschwitz? In *Sophie's Choice*, writer William Styron makes the following observation: 'Auschwitz itself remains inexplicable. The most profound statement yet made about Auschwitz was not a statement at all but a response. The query: 'At Auschwitz, tell me, where was God?' And the answer: 'Where was man?''[3] Ultimately we must accept responsibility for our lives, responding as best we can to the challenges which confront us.

Every one of us must deal with our anger before it deals with us. Frank Vitkovic did not deal with his anger. In the end it dealt with him and brought tragedy into several families and to a whole city. On December 8, 1987, young Frank took a loaded gun, marched into an office building in busy Queen St. Melbourne, and shot dead eight people, most of whom he had not even met. He then leapt from a window to his own death on the pavement several floors below. That day he became the worst mass murderer in the history of the state of Victoria.

In his diary the day he died, Frank wrote these sobering words: 'Today I feel funny. Jitters up my bones all over the place. Palpitations, anger, all that. It's all there. I got too much inside me. Today it must all come out.

'I can't understand my violent impulses. I don't know what's wrong with me. Today I must do it. There's no other way out. I've got to see it through. My head really pounds, I'm all shaky. It's time to die . . . Goodbye all.'

In the end of the two books which housed his diary he wrote: 'I don't care if you make public the contents of this diary. I wrote in part for society to understand how these things happen and how you can pick out people who might be able to do such things. Look for people with a history of rejection, loneliness and ill treatment, who also have a fascination for guns and you won't go wrong.'[4]

An extreme example perhaps, but it does demonstrate the tremendous destructive power which anger can unlock within the human psyche. A great many young people are engaged in gigantic struggles with anger and resentment. They need help in dealing with these emotions and, in order to help them, we must first help ourselves and deal with our own hidden skeletons. At times we are prone to think that the only way to deal with our anger over the events of the past is to vent it on people in the present—often the young.

Failure to confess and deal with anger over the abuses of bygone days is a sure way to guarantee the breakdown of present relationships, especially with those closest to and most reliant upon us. None of us can run from ourselves. Life is too short to blame the world for our problems, and sink into the mire of self-pity and self-condemnation. Let's get on with living.

If you have trouble dealing with pent-up emotions, do yourself and your young friends a favour: Talk it over with someone close to you or seek out a good counsellor for assistance.

Being willing to deal with our own frustrations and hurts will set us free to help young people. Jesus said that it is impossible for you or me to help someone who has a 'speck' in their eye, if we don't recognise and deal first with the 'log' in our own eye (Matt. 7:3-5)!

Having made the commitment to deal with our own insecurities, we can then begin to assist and advise the young without imposing those insecurities on them.

Coach, Don't Control

It's unfortunate, I know, but none of us can protect the young people we care for from the school of hard knocks. There is, and always will be, a certain naivety

172

which goes with being young. To try to protect youth entirely from the pains of life, is to end up manipulating rather than guiding them. No human being wants to be dominated when he or she can be given loving guidance instead. The older a teenager grows, the looser should be your grip on the steering wheel of his or her affairs.

Unless you have prepared them well for life's possibilities, however, you will have set them up for unnecessary hardship. You can ensure that wisdom will temper their eventual independence. As a person of influence in their lives, you can assist them, for example, in the development of problem solving skills.

I cannot help but wonder how many of the young people who attempt suicide in this country each year might not have been spared this, if they had been shown how to solve problems. Parents and youth workers, please don't assume that your teenage children or charges will always, somehow, just muddle through their problems. You as an adult have a greater capacity to get by because you have some life experience behind you. Because of what you've already come through, chances are, no matter how bad things get for you sometimes, you know they will somehow come good in the end. Or, at least, you know that you will pull through intact. But most young people don't have the benefit of your experience. Many of them do not, as yet, possess an adult's level of self-assurance, and, as we've seen, they do face pressures their parents didn't confront at the same age.

Even if your young friends are already in their teens, you can make a start on sharing principles of problem-solving with them. Sit with them. Enquire privately about their problem, asking intelligent questions which show that you are trying to empathise with them. Never trivialise the problem or scoff at their feelings on an issue. Don't lecture them—I know how easy that is to do—but offer guidance and assistance in working out the best course of action for them to take.

Remember always that it is most important for teenagers to learn to solve their own problems and to recognise they have that capacity. They won't always suggest the best responses and that's why your input is so vital as their coach. However, don't get into the habit of wanting to dominate the process and solve their problem for them. After all, you won't always be around to help whenever they face a difficulty in life. Don't set them up for defeat when they're out on their own.

One area where most teenagers want guidance—and many parents feel ill-equipped to provide it—is that of vocation. Parents, youth workers and friends can provide invaluable coaching in the choice of careers. There are several very helpful questions you can encourage a young person to ask when they're trying to decide on a career path:

a) What are the needs of others saying to me? Mother Theresa has been quoted as saying that 'Jesus Christ is thinly disguised in the poor and suffering of the world.' Tony Campolo has it this way: 'Christ stands behind every person in need, waiting to be served by us.' Have a young friend identify which human needs and global problems really tug at his or her heart. This is a good indicator as to the kind of work they will find most fulfilling—work that meets one of these specific needs.

b) What are my gifts and abilities saying to me? Each of us is gifted uniquely and can put those talents to good use. Encourage young friends to identify gifts they might have in relational, intellectual, mechanical and creative and spiritual areas.

174

c) What are my hard times saying to me? Much can be learned about ourselves by the way we react to certain pressure situations. The young should be encouraged not only to identify their strengths, but also their areas of weakness or deficiency. These could be called 'work areas'. Sometimes our past failures can be made into stepping stones to future success, if handled correctly and constructively. The man who wrote the inspirational Christian hymn, *It Is Well With My Soul,* did so at a time of great personal tragedy. Horatio G. Spafford's two daughters—his only children—were drowned when a ship went down one night in very rough seas. His wife and the girls had been travelling from America to what was to be their new home in Israel. Spafford was dealing with some unfinished business and planned to follow them a few weeks later.

When he passed the exact area where his beloved teenage children had died, he went below deck and penned these immortal words: 'When peace, like a river attendeth my way / When sorrows, like the sea billows roll / Whatever my lot, Thou hast taught me to know / "It is well, it is well with my soul." '

Those words have since proved to be of great comfort to troubled people at various times in various parts of the world. We can make constructive use of our weak points.

d) What are my friends saying to me? There is no doubt that we all learn much about ourselves from those around us. What particular vocation we should pursue could be suggested through the comments others have made throughout our lives.

I was always told as a child that I was very artistic, that I possessed a talent for drawing. This assisted me in my choice to study architecture after I left high school. Later on, I decided that God was leading me to become involved in service to the church and the community full-time. Again, I was encouraged in this by people's comments, this time on my public speaking abilities. We can learn a great deal about ourselves from what others tell us—especially those who care about us and believe in us.

e) What might God be calling me to do? If one is a Christian, one can't help but be boosted in one's morale by the thought that there is someone 'up there' who has a definite purpose for one's life. I was created in the image of God. I did not descend from a monkey who got lucky! God has a purpose for my life, which, if I submit myself and my will to his ways, will be made clear to me as I seek to do whatever is put before me now. I will not discover this divine plan by sitting back and waiting for God to do it all, or to reveal it all with writing on some wall! I must get moving in some good endeavour. Only when my car is moving will God steer it in the right direction.

The key is to do something myself. If I think I might be called to be a lawyer, I should do my homework to find out what avenues of study will qualify me and which are the most convenient for me. A firm belief in the sovereignty of God is no excuse for the slovenliness of man.

Remember, parents and leaders, we cannot hope to wipe out our own regrets and painful memories by living things over differently through younger people. The father or mother who didn't ever get to do what they really wanted to do with their lives cannot remedy the situation by engineering the career or marriage path of their son or daughter. The youth worker who regrets his own misspent youth will not help either himself or his youthful charges by dominating or wanting to control their every choice.

Be Smart

When you feel strongly on an issue, try as hard as you can to coax the other person into reaching a good conclusion for themselves. Be smart and let them think it was their own good idea wherever possible.

We will do well as parents, youth workers and friends of young people to learn the difference between authority and influence. There are only two types of power which operate in the affairs of men. If you and I had stood, early one morning nearly 2000 years ago, on the pavement of the Roman praetorium in Jerusalem, we would have witnessed a graphic display of how each works, and how very different they are. The apostle John, writing in the first century, gives us a record of an eyewitness account:

'Then Pilate took him [Jesus] and had him flogged. The soldiers twisted together a crown of thorns and put it on his head. They clothed him in a purple robe and went up to him again and again, saying, "Hail, king of the Jews!" And they struck him in the face.

'Once more Pilate came out and said to the Jews, "Look, I am bringing him out to you to let you know that I find no basis for a charge against him." When Jesus came out wearing the crown of thorns and the purple robe, Pilate said to them, "Here is the Man!" ' (John 19: 1-5).

Pilate's final words here, translated 'Behold the man!' in the King James Version of the Bible, represent a term of disgust. Pilate is pointing to a beaten, bleeding, humiliated and seeming friendless man, and saying to the Jewish religious leaders: 'Do you seriously want me to believe that this man is a threat to the powers of Rome because he claims to be your king? Is this really the best you Jews could do in finding a king to deliver you from Rome? Look at him—it's a pathetic sight! You're pathetic!'

You can imagine Pilate washing his hands not only of Jesus, but of the entire Jewish race, with whom he is well and truly exasperated and for which he has no love at all. History shows him to have been a harsh ruler of Judea, with little tolerance for Jewish law or custom.

There can be no doubt that Pilate did have power over Jesus at this point in time. The cross is proof of that. But we must ask ourselves who had the most effect on human history. Had it not been for his part in the story of Jesus of Nazareth, hardly anyone would ever have heard of Pontius Pilate.

Jesus Christ changed human history. Most of the world today still divides history by reference to his birth. Yet he possessed none of the kind of power Pilate did. What explains His influence? This is where we discover the essential difference between real influence and mere power.

Power is given by a higher human authority. It is most often, though not always, used for manipulating people into doing what someone in power wants them to do. It often uses deceit as a means of winning allegiance. However, it is usually short-lived. Power has a way of corrupting, even the best of men—'absolute power corrupts absolutely'—and, once rulership sinks to become tyranny, people will accommodate it for only so long. Events during the late 1980s in communist lands proved that. Dictators were overthrown in rapid time, as oppressed people turned their bitterness into revolutionary action.

Real influence, on the other hand, is based on authority given from below. God surely had given Christ tremendous gifts which commanded at least the attention, if not the allegiance, of all men. Yet it was because the common people felt His concern, His overriding love for them, that they gave Him the right to influence them. And because this influence was freely given and not demanded, it was a lasting influence for good. Surely this has been the reason for Jesus' inspiring and challenging influence on people right down through the centuries. He did not come wielding a stick, demanding respect; He was our servant, pouring Himself out for our greater good. It is a fact that people will only allow you to influence their lives when they perceive that you have their best interests at heart. Without that permission, you may have power and authority, and you may be gifted to lead, but you will not necessarily have real, lasting, positive influence in people's lives.

There is a key here for all our interpersonal relationships, including our relationships with young people. Parents and leaders, if we seek to dominate, to exercise power over the young, they will inevitably rebel. If, however, we seek to influence by winning their confidence—through caring—we will have greater success in guiding them in the right path.

In the long run, their best interests can only be served when you and I recognise that they have their own destiny to fulfil, their own path to follow. The older they get, the less we can command them, and the more we have to rely on what we've already installed.

And the more we pray!

14

I Don't Need For You To Be Embarrassed About Sex

The Need For Openness

The last thing any teenager needs, as they struggle with their own sexuality, is to be surrounded by adults who cannot deal with 'that' subject without coughing profusely, looking forlornly at the floorboards and turning a rare shade of turquoise. Dr. Bruce Narramore, in his book entitled Adolescence Is Not An Illness, makes the following observation: 'Openness is probably the single most important ingredient of effective sexual education during adolescence."[1]

Open dialogue on the subject of sex has two great benefits for parents and their teenagers. Firstly, it provides good preventative medicine. It's always better to prepare than to have to repair. Better to give your teenagers the information they need in the context of a warm, loving relationship than to have them pick up the 'bare necessities' from the school ground where real love is seldom distinguished from lust.

When you deal openly and sensibly with sex in the home—as a part of day-to-day life and not just in those infrequent 'father and son chats'—you reduce the attraction of dirty jokes for your child. You make language which puts down the opposite sex seem far more offensive in their eyes. You teach that sex is one part—an important part—of a male-female relationship which is spiritual and emotional as well as physical.

For me, there is one very annoying aspect of all the recent talk about 'safe sex'. No-one is telling kids that truly 'safe' sex is safe on levels other than the physical. Sex involves the entire person—body, mind, soul and spirit. You can't just turn one part off in order to satisfy another. They all work together—people's emotions respond to what their bodily senses tell them; the spiritual part of them is either made alive, or destroyed, according to the quality of their thoughts and actions.

With the subject of sex, it's not just what we teach, but how we teach it which is going to determine how younger people treat this fantastic gift from God. If we have shown kids that sex is a subject which we enjoy discussing, yet one which we treat with respect, we will be able to teach how sex fits into life as a whole. So many young adults try to make their whole life fit into sex!

The other great benefit derived from frank discussion about sex is that it indicates trust. The biblical book of Proverbs tells us that whenever you fail to tell someone the truth of a matter, you are actually expressing hatred toward them (Proverbs 26:28).

Strong words, but true. Think about it: If I lie to you about something, I am saying, in a roundabout way, that I don't trust you with the truth. I've probably also been thinking that if I tell it to you as it really is, you might not like me anymore. You may reject me. In thinking this way, I have actually insulted your integrity. If I really love you, I will believe in your capacity to deal appropriately with the truth of the matter.

Are we constantly sending out distress signals to young friends when they come loaded with questions about what makes the world go round? Parents, do you reach for your heart pills everytime your teenager throws a curly question at you? Do you have fainting fits whenever your kids come out with some crude-sounding expression you've never heard before? Remember before you react: They might not even know what it means. If they do, it may be their way of trying to shock you into talking about sex.

Some parents leave 'all that talk about sex' to their local high school. That can be a major mistake. Not least because you as a parent have no guarantee that your children will be taught what you approve of. I was told, just a few days before writing this, about a teacher in a local school who asked her class of young girls if any of them was still a virgin. Only one of the girls, a committed Christian, bravely admitted that she had not been sexually active. The teacher responded to this by saying, as if to embarrass the girl into action: 'Why not? What are you waiting for? Come on, it'll do you good!'

Not all teachers are as overtly slack in the morality department as this one. Teachers, if they are moral and caring people, can be a great help to teenagers in shaping their attitudes toward sexuality. However, in most cases, teachers are not still around a few years down the track, when young adults may need further help or support. But parents usually are.

Our society is in need of sound value-clarification when it comes to sex and relationships in general. The many broken, bruised and hurting lives all around us bear testimony to that. Parents, you can help teenagers to come to grips with their sexuality by being open to their questions, and by accepting responsibility for their development as well-rounded personalities. I'll give some practical pointers on this in just a moment.

First, a word to the church youth leader. The teaching of healthy values should go way beyond just the kids in your church group. One of the greatest things you can offer kids in secular society generally, is practical and relevant instruction on the 'how-to's' of good relationships. When our teeny-bopper magazines are presenting articles on healthy values and priorities, as they are at present, publishers are responding to needs they've identified in their young readers. Magazine publishers spend a good deal of time and money on research to find out what young people want to know, so that their publications can 'scratch' where kids 'itch.' Teenagers are looking for practical principles which will help them develop healthy relationships.

Try getting into your local high school with a well-planned presentation on the subjects of relationship and communication. Design a presentation which can be fitted into the school's human development courses and the like. Avoid overt preaching, but share a practical Christian approach to the dynamics of relationships generally. Deal with all kinds of inter-personal relationships—friendships, marriages and so on. (You would not normally be well advised to talk on sex specifically, or at least, not in any graphic detail). Senior students will particularly benefit from that kind of approach.

I suppose the reason so few parents really equip their teenagers to understand sexuality, is that so few feel adequate to discuss this important subject. After all, if you're an average parent, there are so many specialists out there who could probably do a much better job of it than you, right? Perhaps. But you have an important advantage over the 'experts'—you are related. You have lived with these kids. You know what they're likely to respond to and you will be around to support them as they actually come to grips with their sexuality in everyday life.

'But what if it turns out that my kid knows more about sex than I do?' you're thinking. Take heart—the basics haven't really changed at all! Whatever you do, don't make the mistake of thinking that all your teenagers need to know are the physical mechanics of sex. They may already know that much. If you buy someone a rifle, you don't just teach that person how to pull the trigger, you make sure the recipient understands all the ramifications of the new power he or she possesses. So what do young people need to know aside from the physical side of sex?

Sex is more than an act

A magazine advertisement published by the Australian National Council on AIDS features a full-page photo of a condom with the caption: 'Only one thing stands between you and AIDS.' The paragraph beneath reads in part: 'So next time you go to bed with someone, take out a little life insurance. Use a condom. Apart from saying "no" it's the only thing that stands between you and AIDS.'[2]

This reflects another form of AIDS which is crippling whole families: Acquired *Integrity* Deficiency Syndrome. Many people refuse to tell youth the whole truth about sex. For sex to be truly safe, it must be safe on more than just the physical level. It must be safe emotionally, psychologically and spiritually—protected by the covering of a trusting and loyal relationship.

One British sex therapist has this to say on the subject: 'Sex is not an appetite like hunger. Our sexuality is not a

185

disembodied drive separate from the rest of our human characteristics, nor just an "aspect" of our personalities. Rather, sex is us. Though there is much more to us than our sexuality, to be fully human as God meant us to be, we must acknowledge our sexuality as an integral part of our being.'[3]

Sexual experience goes to the very basis of all that we are. Sexual intercourse is more than a physical entry of one person's body into another's—it also features an 'entering' of one person's emotional life into the other's. This, says Richard J. Foster, is part of the reason why masturbation will not fully satisfy: 'It perpetuates the myth of the self-contained lover.'[4]

'The sexual delusion of our time is that sexuality is only about orgasms,' writes Lewis Smedes. 'The evil that this distortion does is many sided.'[5] Sex seen as merely a physical act can actually get in the way of a relationship! People sometimes wake up one morning to find their lover of years has left them. They are taken totally by surprise, devastated by this desertion, basically because they didn't see it coming. What they had thought was an intimate relationship was really only a physical one. Ultimately there was no giving, only taking.

Sex is not a dirty thing and it's not cheap

A Christian view of sex is based on the life and teachings of Jesus. Some people mistakenly believe that Christ had little to say about sexuality. In fact, Jesus not only gave us the most comprehensive body of teaching on relationships generally, he also boldly stood against the stereotypes of his day to leave us a radical example of how we should treat one another. In summary: 'What Jesus did for human sexuality was considerable

... Running bluntly against both Jewish and Gentile culture, He publicly displayed a tenderness and concern for women that demonstrated His respect for them as persons ... He undermined legalistic morality by recalling that the heart had its own kind of sex life. ... He showed that marriage and sex were planted in the Garden of Eden, reminding us that God intended from the beginning that men and women should be attracted to one another and that sexuality therefore was not one of the nasty products of sin, but the exciting dynamic of creation.'[6]

On the basis of all that Jesus taught and demonstrated about human relationships, there are some very positive things we can teach our kids about sex and sexuality. Firstly, there is the incalculable value of each individual person. Having been created in the image of God, every son or daughter of Adam is special to Him and is therefore deserving of respect and consideration. Consequently, no person deserves to be manipulated or used to meet another's needs. 'Do unto others as you would have them do unto you' sums it up very well indeed!

Alongside His belief in the dignity and inherent worth of every human being, Jesus also held that man is sinful. His teaching encapsulated and developed further all that the Old Testament prophets had to say on the subject of humanity's fall from grace. In the heart of every man and woman born is a basic bias toward rebellion against God and all that is right. According to the Bible, only Jesus, the Son of God, born of a virgin, escaped this hereditary cycle of sinfulness. As the perfect and pure man He alone was qualified to die for humanity's sins rather than His own. At one point in the gospels we are told that Jesus knew 'what was in the heart of man' and refused to trust His destiny purely into the hands of his adoring public—He knew how fickle we can be.

Secondly then, we should teach the young never to underestimate the capacity of the human being to do the wrong thing. When a man and woman place themselves in a compromising position, they will be tempted and in such a setting, when hormones are prone to take over, innocent intentions do not guard against hurtful actions. This is one reason why drugs and alcohol are such a bad idea—they weaken the resolve to say 'no'!

We should also make our youth aware that the other party in any 'close encounter' is also human and has the same capacity to do the wrong thing. 'He'd never do anything to hurt me!' she exclaims. 'He loves me too much!' 'She'd never let me go too far,' says he confidently, 'she's too spiritual for that!'

Parents and leaders, be honest with teenagers about the full potency of the human sexual drive. Don't hide the power of sexual chemistry away behind simplistic romantic talk. Romance is great—it's really one of the big things which gets people to the altar. But you can't go the rest of your life living off romance. There has to be more in the relationship if it is to last. Recent surveys have demonstrated that longevity in marriages is most common among those who were not sexually active with each other prior to marriage. I would suggest that this is because, in the former cases, the value of commitment is understood, and commitment is what we all really want from our partners.

In Bruce Springsteen's song, *Cautious Man*, the key character, a rover named Billy Horton, is happy to live his life alone and carefree until one day the unthinkable happens—he meets Miss Right and falls in love. He begins to plan his life around his new love, dreaming of settling down and building her a home. Basically he just wants to do all the things lovers do together. Unfortunately, Billy is afraid of commitment, having tasted so little of it in the past. Poetically the song says that on one hand he tattoos the word 'love' and on the other hand the word 'fear'—which hand holds his fate, he is not sure. Billy wants to make a real and lasting commitment, sensing that this is the right way to go, yet his heart is afraid. Perhaps afraid that he might fail and hurt the one he loves; perhaps afraid that he may be the one who gets hurt. Billy knows that 'in the restless heart the seeds of betrayal lay.' His dilemma is real and it is one shared by many young people today.

Without commitment sex is dangerous. It is dangerous because it promises what it cannot deliver—true intimacy. John Smith, in writing about the trend these days for people to opt out of a marriage citing incompatability as the cause, makes this very good point: 'I seriously doubt that there is any such thing as incompatability. There are poor choices, difficult options, less-than-ideal foundations of common interest—but lasting and fulfilling relationships are a matter of mutual commitment. . . The problem with modern marriage is that we expect too much and give too little.'[7]

It is absolutely vital too, to pass on to teenagers an appreciation of having a wide circle of friends. So many young people get into problems associated with sex simply because they narrow their options down too quickly—they abandon other friendships, giving all their attention to one relationship. One of the greatest benefits for the young in belonging to a strong, vibrant local church is that there they have the opportunity to form friendships with a wide variety of people, not just those on their own peer or interest group. A multiplicity of friendships with members of both sexes, provides a valuable opportunity for young people to discover themselves and to find out what it is they are looking for in their closest relationships.

All of us have reference groups—people we go to for advice, people whose example we follow and whose approval we value. They are a powerful influence on us for right or wrong, depending on who we 'hang out' with. Encouraging young people we care about to find and keep contact with positive reference groups is one of the greatest favours we can do them. Parent, you cannot choose your teenagers' friends—try it and see how far you get! Yet you can lead them to an appreciation of healthy peer groups.

You can also help teenagers to appreciate the resources on hand outside the home when they need advice or guidance. There will be times when they will not particularly want to talk to you about a relationship, but they will want to share with someone. If you have led them to appreciate church leaders, good teachers, community workers and the like, you have made things much easier for them. If you spend all your time in the home running down every authority structure out there, your kids will pick up on your apparent distrust and will miss out on a valuable resource.

3. Sex is no substitute for God!

It is interesting to see that, in an age where so many people have abandoned belief in God, in His place men and women have often made a lover the object of their highest devotion. Sex has become an act of worship, an exercise in the kind of spiritual transcendence which once characterised divine worship. People seem to need 'salvation,' even when they don't believe in God.

Dr. Anthony Campolo makes this point well: 'It is possible for a person to "fall in love" in such a way as to make his/her partner into a messiah who provides deliverance, at least temporarily, from the pangs of human existence.'

He goes on to cite the way we talk about love and lovers in our popular music. 'Understandably, most love songs in our culture depict lovers in sublime language and utilise a vocabulary traditionally reserved for religion. The music of romance is prone to have such phrases as: "I can't get along without you baby," "You're my everything," "I'm nothing without you." '

This idolising of one's partner does however, as Campolo points out, have its own hidden dangers. 'The person is completely lost in the lover and believes that there is no meaning apart from being with that person forever.' Once the illusion is shattered, once the woman comes to discover that her lover is not the knight in shining armour, or the guy realises he's involved with something less than an angel, the whole thing comes tumbling down. 'Unfortunately, lovers almost always betray our idealisation of them. They are too available for scrutiny ... No-one, save Jesus, is capable of maintaining the image of divinity upon close inspection.'[8]

As we have already seen, Australia is a nation with a massive problem in the area of marriage breakdown. In one year, the Commonwealth Government spent $1.8 billion on divorce and only $500,000 on marriage counselling. Yet, for most Australians, marriage is still a thing to be valued. Many attest to this by going through with marriage a second or third time, pursuing the ideal partnership despite past failures. Bruce Wilson says, in *Can God Survive In Australia.*: 'My suspicion is that detailed Australian research would probably rank the family, together with upward social and material mobility, first in what Australians really live for.' Could it be that, rather than expecting too little from marriage and family we are actually expecting too much from them? 'For Christians, marriage and the family are God-given. For modern Australians, they tend to become God.'[9]

At the bottom of all this, is the human being's need to be loved and to be given identity. At a time when work and religion are offering less purpose and meaning in the eyes of the average Australian, many turn to marriage and family for these transcendent values.

It seems that, through the sciences, we have come to know so much about how human beings are made up. We have defined what people are, at least biologically. We use this extensive knowledge to build technological gadgets which can make life more comfortable for mankind. Yet it seems for all our learning, we have been unable to produce in a laboratory or factory the two things men and women crave most—love and purpose. Life may be seen more comfortable than it was back in the days when more people truly believed in God, but it is certainly no more meaningful. In our quest to learn about and control the outer environment, we have put aside what we learned long ago about the inner environment: that 'the human creature infinitely longs to be loved rather than to be defined.'[10]

No human being or institution can give us the type of total, unconditional, unyielding love and security which we crave. Only God can fill that need in the soul.

Jesus taught that love for others, our neighbours (including wives and husbands), can only flow from us when we have known the love of God—when we have experienced the security and strength of His compassion for us. Having tasted the warmth of His love, we can be renewed daily in this experience through fellowship with him, and can thus be equipped to find love in our hearts for others. When respect for His ways and wishes is paramount for us, life will work as it was first intended to.

We should make sure our young friends realise that God—who invented sex and knows how to make it a real 'buzz'—intended that the commitment of marriage would provide a covering, a 'safety net' for sexual activity, which ensures that neither party feels used by the other. But, this will only occur if the marriage is a three-way partnership: a husband, a wife, and God, the source of all love.

The greatest way to teach teenagers a healthy respect for sex is, of course, by example, through our own behaviour and relationships. Which brings us to the next section.

15

I Learn More By Watching You Than Listening To You

The Need For Sincerity

If there is one last thing I think every parent and youth worker needs to know about teenagers, it is this: Young people know whether the instruction you give them actually lines up with the way in which you conduct your life. High schoolers in some places have a saying: 'Get real!' This is great advice for those of us who want to make a positive mark on today's youth.

Get Real!

Sincerity would have to be one of the most vital attributes needed for developing relationships with teenagers. Young people can be very adept at spotting shallow insincerity in others. Teenagers can be naive, but they are less so about their families than they might sometimes be about their friends and aquaintances outside the home. They tend to be harsher in their judgement of those they live with, than they are toward their peers.

The word 'sincere' is an interesting one in itself—it is derived from two Latin words, *sin cera*. In ancient

Roman times, if you were wanted to make a good impression on the Joneses next door, you would probably do so by adding to your front lawn an expensive marble statue, which had been handcrafted by some gifted local artisan. People cruising by on their late model chariots or camels (with twin overhead humps) could not help but be impressed by your obvious good taste and buying power.

The problem with marble statues is that they can be chipped. One day, when the kids down the street are playing Ben Hur, one of them happens to run his skateboard a little too closely by your treasured art piece, and collects a hunk of marble en route. You are understandably distraught—this glorified garden gnome cost you an arm and a leg. You can't just Superglue the whole thing back together because Superglue hasn't been invented yet. Your only recourse is to call the local waxman.

The waxman arrives at your door carrying his familiar pot of smelly wax, which he heats and colours in situ to match the shade of marble chosen by your sculptor. He fills in the broken section with coloured wax and, when he's through, you can't even tell that the statue was ever broken—not from a distance anyway. On closer inspection you notice that, alas, things are not all they appear to be.

'What's all this got to do with sincerity?' I hear you ask. The term sin cera simply means 'without wax.' It's important for us all, every so often, to ask ourselves: Am I 'real' up close? Do I tend to align my actions with a different set of ethics to those I espouse with my mouth? Do I practise what I preach? There are, I think, four areas in which sincerity is important to a young person:

Your Responses To Members Of The Opposite Sex

Parents, much of what your sons or daughters know about how they should treat members of the opposite sex, they have learned from you. From early childhood they have learned to mimic you. As they hasten now toward adulthood, they look more than ever to their parents for clues about how to get on in the wide world of interpersonal relationships.

In our marriages, in particular, we need to demonstrate a healthy respect for members of the opposite sex. That sounds a little vague, so let's break it down into more practical terms.

As far as I can see, in every marriage that succeeds there are some common principles at work. In fact, 'work' is the operative word here for, as Dr. Billy Graham has said, 'A marriage is two people working hard together all of the time.'

First, in marriages which succeed, the husband is aware of his proper role. Basically, I think the man of the house needs to be four things in the marriage relationship: a lover, a leader, a provider and a protector. Sadly, too many Australian males are not able to fulfil the first aspect because they have trouble with vulnerability. They seem able to express their innermost feelings only when they've 'had a few', when alcohol has loosened up the emotive part of them. This is tragic.

From early childhood males in this country are taught —by implication if not by word—that men don't cry. As a result emotions in a man are perceived, at least by a great many men, as being a sign of weakness, of unmanliness. The extreme outworking of all this is the machoism which has pervaded some parts of Aussie male-dom. A worse caricature of strong manhood one would be hard pressed to find. The macho man is heavy-handed in his dealings with women; he is limited in his vocabulary, placing great store on invective; he'll fight first and ask questions later, or so he says.

Machoism is the extreme response to the outside world of men who don't feel very good about themselves. It is a defensive position to take. In short, it is the antithesis of vulnerability.

Modern marriages, modern kids, definitely need men who know how to be vulnerable. One survey asked men what they found hardest to say, particularly to women. The most popular responses are revealing: most of those men surveyed said they found it most difficult to say things such as 'I'm sorry,' 'I was wrong' and 'I need your help.' John Smith, founder of the God Squad motor cycle club, and a man known for his empathy and concern for the Aussie male, has said that he owes his father a huge debt for teaching him how to cry. I second that. My father raised seven children. He was always the sole breadwinner and worked two jobs for most of my childhood—one on weekdays and another on Friday nights and Saturday mornings. Yet he still had time, somehow, to play hide and seek or *Monopoly* with his kids, or to kick a football with us. He's been a good provider, a good man. Yet he knew how to cry when the occasion called for it. I vividly recall seeing him at times kneeling by his bed, praying and crying for someone in need or some situation in the family.

Only when he has learned to be vulnerable can the man of the house become a real lover. Studies conducted throughout one year in the US, showed that there were basically twelve causes of divorce in that year. But top of the list was communication breakdown, followed by 'sexual incompatibility.' It is hardly surprising that sex should rate so highly, but few would predict that communication would come in first.

Without openness there can be no communication between people, and without communication even sex is far less than it could be. Without the decision to become emotionally vulnerable, or 'hurtable', to place oneself at risk in the hands of another, sex is little more than using someone else to satisfy one's own physical needs. Many wives feel cheated because their husbands only seem to want mechanical sex, without intimacy.

When a man begins to really communicate he will often inspire the respect he craves from his wife. This is what biblical leadership in the home is about—not one member calling all the shots, dominating proceedings and insisting like a spoilt child on having his own way—but setting a pace which the other partner will want to follow. The husband is, in other words, to bring out the best in his wife.

Husbands need also to be providers. How many marriages have been shipwrecked, how many children's lives washed up, against the rocks of male irresponsibility with money? I'll never forget reading a letter given to me by a 15-year-old schoolgirl on one of my trips to a particular Asian country. This young lady had become a Christian during a series of concerts we were holding in a growing city church. Her letter told a story of heartache which resulted from her accidental discovery that she had been adopted as a baby.

While this helped to explain some of the tensions she was now experiencing with her parents, brothers and sisters, it also created a whole range of new problems not the least of which was the gnawing self-doubt and bitter resentment she now carried in her heart.

It was the last paragraph of the letter that moved me most. It told of the circumstances surrounding her adoption. She had been conceived at a time when her natural father was heavily in debt because of his gambling activities. He had sold all that he could and was now facing violence at the hands of his creditors. So he set up an arrangement whereby he would sell his child into adoption.

As a result of one man's financial incompetence, this young teenager had borne long-standing feelings of bitterness and hatred. Only a powerful experience with the love of Christ, and the help of a good church, were able to transform her. How many other young men and women are grappling with similar feelings, but without the kind of assistance this girl received?

Not only does a husband need to be able to provide monetarily, he must also provide opportunities for his wife—opportunities to develop her own gifts and potentialities. Many a man feels threatened by gifted women and thus seeks to stifle his wife's development in areas where she has talent. He should be her greatest encourager and admirer.

Husbands need to protect their wives. I don't wish to imply that, without a male to protect her, a woman will never be able to make her way in the world. But I have spoken to many a young woman who, looking for a potential life partner, complains that every man she meets is a real wimp! Guys, the issue here is not whether or not we pump iron and have the body mass of a medium-sized orang-outang—it's whether or not we have the 'intestinal fortitude' to stand for what we believe, to protect those we care about. This issue of protection goes beyond the physical dimension. There is an emotional and psychological dimension too. We can, through our own strength of character and sensitivity to our partner's needs, offer solace and comfort in the

200

midst of life's often harsh realities.

In all of this, we fathers pass on to our sons more information than we realise, about how the women of our world ought to be, deserve to be, treated.

Likewise, mothers, you too have a role to play in helping to shape your daughters' perceptions of manhood. Through the years, many have tried to discredit the Bible's teaching on the role of women in the home and in society. They've attempted to paint it as an antiquated, anti-female code, designed by men for the benefit of men. A closer look at it might render a different response.

In biblical teaching, a wife is to be prized by her spouse. He is to love her with the same energy of love with which Christ loved the Church. He is told that if he mistreats her, his prayers will be hindered—his whole relationship with God is on shaky ground—and he will stand under sentence of judgement. Strong words!

The wife is to respond to her husband's lead—his commitment and vulnerability— by respecting him and building him up. This is one of the most powerful things any woman can do for her man—encourage him. Today there are so many infiuences which are seeking to drag men down, that any positive input their wives can offer will make a huge difference in their self-esteem.

Submission in the biblical sense has nothing to do with being trodden under foot. It has to do with loyalty. Loyalty is doing what is in the other person's best interests at all times; making the other person look good, even when doing so costs you something. A wife who is constantly arguing with her husband simply for the sake of it, is risking losing his love for good. She has also given her children a big lesson in ultra-feminism.

I have no doubt that, to a point, feminism is a very

good thing. In so far as it has improved and continues to enhance the lot of women in society, opening opportunities which are rightly theirs, it is a godsend for all humankind. It brings us closer to what God first intended for humanity. In God's order, neither man nor woman was created to be inferior to the other—just different, and very interesting to one another.

There is, as with all good things, however, an extreme to which feminist ideas can be taken. Radical extremists in feminist movements have enlisted a great deal of media interest in their various causes. As a result of such propaganda, some males now feel very tentative when trying to relate to women, because they are overly sensitive about sexism. Many a woman is also more disadvantaged than helped by radical feminism, because when she tries to extend herself and fulfil her potential, suspicions arise among her male counterparts—and not a few female ones—about her real motives. Some suspect her being ultra-feminist, when she simply wants to utilise her gifts, achieving all that she is capable of.

I would humbly offer just one piece of advice to my sisters reading this. If you have been hurt by a man or men, try not to pass your hurt on to your daughters by generalising about the deficiencies of the male race. This will rob them of happy and meaningful relationships later on.

In summary, parents, I think we owe it to our kids to be truly accessible, one with the other, in a marriage partnership. We must expose our hearts and minds to one another. Unless we can do this with each other, we will have a very hard time doing it with our children and at the same time we will be painting a very bad portrait of what life with the opposite sex is really all about.

Your Responses To Drugs Of Various Kinds
Studies by governments in various parts of the world, have revealed that a majority of teenagers who drink alcohol had their first experiences with it in the company, and with the approval, of their parents or guardians. Australia already has a growing problem with youth alcoholism, and some unwise parents apparently have much to answer for.

In a similar way, young people whose parents have a history of abusing pills and medication—millions place an unhealthy reliance on barbituates or amphetamines to help them through each day—very often find it much harder to say 'no' when offered drugs. The abuse of, or reliance upon, chemicals has simply formed a part of their childhood environment.

Your Attitudes To Material And Spiritual Things
Some adults bemoan what they see as the materialistic mindset of the typical modern teenager, without seeing how such attitudes are learned from older generations.

The past 20 years has seen the emergence in the developed world of what is perhaps the most narcissistic generation in history. We are obsessed with ourselves and 'actualising our inner potential.' We buy material things which give us pleasure and free us from mundane, tedious tasks, so that we have more time to spend on 'the most important people in the world'—us. In our preoccupation with self, we are often numb to the problems of the world outside our own socio-economic enclave.

According to Richard J. Barnet, the economic and political analyst, 'More food is produced [around the world today] than ever before. There have been dramatic increases in yields. A growing middle class around the world is eating better. But the hunger is also increasing." Something like 25% of the world's population uses up 80% of its resources. There are now 800 million people living in absolute poverty throughout the world—that is to say, they earn less than $90 per family per year. Half of their children die before the age of five years and they have little hope of a brighter future. 10,000 children die each day in developing countries, from diseases which could have been prevented with immunisation. Another 40,000 children under five years die daily of malnutrition. The sorry list of statistics goes on.

Through selfish living, many of us comparatively rich westerners not only rob our poorer brother, we rob ourselves. Jesus taught that a self indulgent value system may, for a time, produce sensual enjoyment, but it will also eventually lead to spiritual impoverishment. Nowhere did He demonstrate this more graphically than in the parable of the prodigal son (Luke 15).

The young man in the narrative has left the simple life on the farm, to take up a much more cosmopolitan existence in the big city. He has demanded his share of the family inheritance, due to him at his father's death, and has converted it into hard cash.

What follows is a sorry tale of the fickleness of wealth and the friendships it generates. Eventually, his money spent and his fair weather friends gone, the young man is scratching out a living, feeding pigs. It was not with the loss of his fortune that his troubles began, however. His downhill slide had already commenced at the beginning of the story, where his first words to his father revealed where his priorities lay. 'Father,' he said, 'Give me what belongs to me.'

We live in a 'give me' world today. Like the son in this

story, we pay for pleasure and, in the process, often swap the timeless for the transitory. Our values become strangely distorted, our priorities tragically confused, and our lives are made the poorer as a result. What's more, we pass on to the next generation a lifestyle which is empty of real meaning.

Now, neither you nor I, on our own, can ever hope to remedy the massive social ills which afflict our world today. Political systems, economic structures, bureaucracies and many other factors come into play when we talk about feeding the starving, restoring the dispossessed and healing the diseased.

Together we can, however, make a difference if we are prepared to make adjustments to our own lifestyles. We can determine to share our resources instead of hoarding them. In so doing, we will help even out some of the inequalities which exist in our world, and we will be teaching young people around us to do the same. The youth of today are, after all, the greatest resource for future change. Our world needs less yuppies—young urban professionals—and more yummies—young urban missionaries.

We can make a start by taking on a more simple personal life style. Jesus taught his first 'missionaries' in Mark chapter 6 to travel light. They were instructed to take nothing extra for their journey, just whatever they needed to be effective. God has no problem with money, but he does seem to have a major diffculty with greed. In Beyond Renewal, Brian Hathaway asks us to imagine that our boss has just granted us a $100 a week pay rise. 'Most of us,' he states, 'would have probably adjusted our lifestyle to the previous salary and been seeking to live within it. Now we have an increase, 'Great, we can get the extra things we have been wanting.' So . . . we enhance our lifestyle to accommodate the extra that we are earning.'[2] We would do better to find more creative ways of using our excess.

We can model sensible buying habits, by resisting slick salesmanship and its twin, clever advertising. Many people are conned into buying what they don't really need. There is a whole field of psychology now devoted to the science of selling. Drawn in by subtle environmental conditioning techniques—for example, the use of 'muzak' to relax shoppers—people leave the stores with more unnecessary things with which to clutter their lives.

We can train ourselves and teenage friends to reject credit as much as possible. Once upon a time, we would be willing to wait for something, if we couldn't afford to buy it immediately. These days, we don't need to wait. Credit has enabled us to buy now and pay later. Unfortunately, we pay more later. Throughout this nation, people of all ages are getting into trouble, through overcommitting themselves on credit.

The young are perhaps suffering the most. At whom do most of the advertisers aim their slick promises, and who do they bait with their credit schemes? The young. The young have money, and they like spending it. They use it as a means of expressing their independence. A growing number of young adult bankrupts now rue the day they signed on the dotted line. Hathaway says: 'Oh, for a generation of Christian young people who rise up and say, "Enough of this frenzy." Could this happen? Don't hold your breath. Young people do not have many adult models to follow in this regard.'[3]

Finally, we can set a good example by learning to give. We can involve teenagers in giving to feeding programmes and job creation schemes. We can encourage support of church-based missions programmes which adopt a holistic approach to meeting world needs—spiritual, physical, emotional and social.

Many of us give one-off or infrequent monetary gifts, but more is achieved by regular giving which comes out of a well researched and heartfelt commitment. Parents, by allowing teenagers to participate in choosing which people or projects to support, and in deciding where spending cuts can be made at home, you can teach them the art of intelligent giving.

We can model the giving of time too. Parents taking up local community support work of some kind, is a great way for you to demonstrate concern for the wider human family. High schools often have parents' groups which are involved in some kind of community endeavour. Groups which do more than service the needs of those on the committee are the ones to look for.

Young people should be encouraged to make the best possible use of their school holidays. Perhaps, if you're a parent, you might encourage your teenagers to sign up for local community service of some kind, or join with a foreign aid agency or church missions organisation for a short temm aid project. Visiting a Third World country is an eye-opener for any westernised young person.

If you're a youth leader or student worker, why not organise a summer holiday aid programme? Link up with a foreign aid or missions agency, and take a small team overseas for a few weeks. You cannot do this kind of work on your own, as young people need to be properly prepared for any overseas service. They need to understand at least something of the culture of the country they will be visiting and must be taught that they are going to serve, to learn and to give. (Paternalism is deadly to care programmes.)

Many church youth workers in Australia go on holidays for the whole of the summer season and in so doing miss some of the greatest opportunities to be of real service to the community and the world. Every year, the rate of juvenile crime in this country climbs markedly around January which, of course, is when young people are starting to look for things to keep them interested during the long summer vacation. Many youth pastors seem to be more interested in their vacation than their vocation. School and university holidays are a great time for involving young people in hands-on ministry to needy people groups.

I was 27 years of age when I visited Sri Lanka, the beautiful island known for its tea plantations and lush tropical scenery. It changed me. I will never forget the beggars I saw. Sitting on their small mats, they lined the streets of the over crowded cities. Some carried deformities which had been inflicted on them in childhood, by parents who knew that crippled beggars made more money.

If this kind of travel so affected me in my mid-20s, I can only imagine what a strong impact it would have on the mind of a teenager. I'm not speaking here about tourism, you understand. I'm talking about going somewhere to serve in some specific task—it might be building a hospital, or ploughing a field.

In short then, whether you are a parent, youth worker, or concerned friend, you can be instrumental in demonstrating a radical lifestyle for teenagers who desperately want a challenge, and really want to make a difference in their world. Provoke the rebel within young people. Get them moving against the inequalities of the status quo. Show them how to handle the responsibility which comes with material prosperity.

Your Response To Conflict

As painful as it may be for you to concede, it is inevitable that a certain amount of unpleasant conflict will arise in the lives of the kids you love. All relationships between human beings are prone to experience tension and stress at times. Even the healthiest relationships owe their success not so much to the absence of conflict, as to the proper management of it. One of the most important keys to forming lasting relationships is the practise of self-control.

In the Bible, 1 Timothy 3:2 has some vital counsel concerning leadership. It tells us that leaders are to be 'temperate.' That word literally means moderate, not given to hasty actions, not explosive or rash. We are all leaders in one way or another—others are watching us—and we would do well to model this attitude for young people around us.

The Bible makes it clear that we need God's help to achieve real self-control. The Christian believer can call on the power of God's Holy Spirit for help when self-discipline is difficult. Moderation is called a 'fruit of the Holy Spirit.'

Get Out Of My Face!

Let me offer some quick pointers on resolving conflict with teenagers.

Respect The Individual. Don't try to deal with conflict by arming yourself with 'ammunition' against the other person in advance.

Deal With A Problem In The Proper Time And Setting. If a problem needs to be dealt with on the spot, deal with it quickly. If it does not require immediate action, set aside a convenient time to talk it through calmly and reasonably. Make an 'appointment' to talk over the problem together in an uncluttered environment, free from interruptions.

Agree To Be Open To The Other Person's Point Of View. Before talking things out, agree that no-one will express their opinion without first repeating, in their own words, what the other thinks and feels in the situation.

Build On Areas Where You Both Agree. Don't allow these positive areas to be overshadowed by ones where views differ.

Compromise If You Can. Look for a mutually satisfying compromise wherever possible. As an adult concerned for the welfare of the kids you care about, you will want (and need) to maintain and insist upon certain standards, but be flexible in areas where our standards are open to question.

Agree To Disagree Where Necessary. If, after a caring and thorough discussion of the issues, no agreement or suitable compromise is reached, try to maintain respect for the other person's right to choose for himself or herself.

Younger people are learning from us all the time. The good, the bad, and the ugly parts of our lives are all on show to those young people who are close to us. We need to work as hard as we can to live by the principles we espouse to them, to meet the standards we have set for them. Our example may, in the long run, have more influence than our words.

16

Heroic Christianity

The Challenge For The Church
There is certainly a good deal the Church needs to do if it is to redress its ignorance of where young people are at today. Some sections of the Church seem to be losing touch with the young, at a time when teenagers most need their influence. There are basically four things Christians can do to improve the Church's relations with modern youth.

Be Relevant
Ask just about any group of secondary school students what they think about the Church, and you'll learn that either it's not a subject they've thought about, or they find the Church irrelevant to them and their situation. Who can blame them for thinking this way, when all most kids ever hear about the Church, courtesy of the mass media, is that it hasn't yet decided whether or not it needs women priests? No, I'm not trying to trivialise that issue, which is an important one to many Christians in certain denominations. But to teenagers out there, this issue is hardly relevant to daily life. It is an internal

one, it makes no impression, for better or worse, on their own world.

The Church's fear of change has played a major role in keeping it irrelevant to large sections of the Australian population. The Church around the world now faces the challenge of remaining relevant and contemporary in a rapidly changing world. We might as well get used to change, and learn how to deal with its quick pace—it isn't about to slow down in the near future.

Some Christian leaders have retreated from the real world and its issues because they've grown afraid of its influence on the Church. Doubtless, there are issues confonting today's Christendom which are both unique to this time in history, and difficult to respond to. Never before has the Church of Jesus Christ needed to dig into the word of God, and seek His will on bended knee, as it does on such modern problems as those raised by IVF technology, AIDS infection and the like. Simple answers may not be forthcoming. We must be sensitive to God's standards and compassionate toward mankind, just as our Lord would be.

My point is that we often hear Christians bemoaning the influence of humanists in government or the media, or commiserating with each other about occultists who pray against the Church. Yet, if we are to take the Bible seriously at all, we would have to say that the Church, rather than being on the back foot, ought to be on the offensive. Jesus taught that it was to grow, extending the kingdom of God, the rule of God, in human affairs.

Unfortunately, sometimes the Church takes itself and its traditions too seriously, and the simple power of its gospel not seriously enough. Whenever this happens, the Church becomes pharisaical. Jesus had major problems with the Pharisees of his day, the representatives of the predominant religious class, because, he said, they preferred the traditions of men to the commandments of God (Mark 7:6-8). Tradition can, of course, be a valuable and enriching part of faith. But when we worship man's traditions we can grow deaf to the onward call of God's Spirit and die spiritually. We need frequently to look at tradition and decipher what God has given us, and expects us to hold onto, and what is arbitrary. The seven last words of a dying church, said one writer, are: 'It has never been done this way before.'

During my second speaking tour of England, I was privileged to visit a very interesting church in the city of Manchester. The people met in a simple, unadorned hall which was situated in a poor part of town and surrounded by high-rise government housing estates. I was told that the units were occupied by low income families, mainly single mothers with teenage children.

After our meeting, the pastor's wife told me a remarkable story. Apparently, when she and her husband first arrived to take on the pastorate, they found a church which was deeply entrenched in conservatism. Its people had adopted a very insular approach to the community. Rather than constantly trying to find new ways to reach out, they clung to methods and forms of the past, ignoring the needs of the real world outside their door. They seemed more concerned with maintaining their own status quo, than being of benefit to the community.

In sheer frustration, the pastor one day took to the wooden pulpit with an axe. A short while later, he removed the old pews and changed the seating arrangement, making it more informal. Both the pews and the pulpit had been in the hall since the church was pioneered decades earlier. He saw them as symbols of a bygone era and was determined to bring the people up-to-date with the world outside. For his efforts, he came in for some strong criticism and a number of key church members left. This man recognised that, from time to time, the Church must change if it is to affect its society.

When I spoke in that Manchester church, my audience were mainly teenagers from low income families, who lived in the housing estates nearby. A willingness to change was breathing new life into that fellowship. It was once more doing something constructive, reaching out to the people who needed its help most. The gospel was once again allowed to do its work, changing and healing broken lives. It is, after all, the gospel that is the 'power of God unto salvation' (Romans 1:16), and not the rituals or practices of any church.

If the Church of today is to reach the youth of our society, it must be more relevant in the style of its expression. Even a cursory glance at the history of the Church, will reveal that whenever the Church has made inroads into its culture, it has done so because men and women of God have been prepared to adjust their style in order to be understood by their society. And they did this without compromising their message.

Several centuries ago, a young Isaac Watts decided that the religious songs of his day did not say anything to him or his generation. So he wrote his own songs, and they've become some of our finest hymns. John Wesley determined that hearing the gospel of Christ was not solely the right of the pious, class-conscious, upper strata of English society. He translated it into words and songs which the common people could understand. Young men and women were drawn to Christ in the thousands during the Methodist revival which followed. William Booth didn't settle for comfortable Christianity either.

His down-to-earth style and real world vision were not appreciated in the churches, so he took his music and preaching to the streets, where they were accepted with open arms. The Salvation Army was born.

As it was in Booth's day, so it is in ours. We have no right to let the teenagers of today just walk by churches without giving a thought to the claims of Christ. Church leaders need to modify their preaching style wherever it does not relate; churches need to change their musical forms where they remain inaccessible to the masses; churches need to improve their advertising. Whether the Church likes it or not, it is competing for attention, and it has to work hard at it because so many young people don't think the Church has anything to say to them.

The Church also needs to become more relevant in the substance of what it has to say. More than ever, Christian communicators need to combine philosophy with practicability in their work. Young people are searching for workable practical values; they are hungry for real answers, not abstract musings drawn from dusty books.

The Church needs to listen to young people and discover what it is they are looking for. What questions are they asking? What unique and pressing dilemmas do they face? In order to make ourselves more relevant to the young, we will need to begin to listen to the things they listen to. Pastors ought to tune their radios to the FM stations which pitch their product at the youth market. One pastor, who leads a large suburban congregation, tried this and later testified that it had given him a whole new compassion for teenagers.

Church leaders must watch some of the things young people are watching, to familiarise themselves with the film, TV and video market. Fortunately, leaders, you don't need to see every movie that hits the town to know what they are basically saying to kids. You will find plenty of magazines and newspapers which feature reviews and synopses.

Leaders, read some of the material kids are reading. Popular teen magazines come from a number of genres —there are music magazines which cater for every conceivable taste, movie and TV magazines, and magazines aimed at one or other of the sexes. Buying a magazine now and again will help keep you in touch.

But the best research has, and always will, come out of time spent with real people. Why was Jesus so relevant to the common people who 'heard him gladly' (Mark 12:37)? It was because He mixed with real people in everyday situations. His illustrative material was drawn from the normal, the commonplace. He knew the people He was speaking to because He lived among them. The best kind of research into youth issues is drawn from sharing their lives, their experiences, listening to their problems, being exposed to their world.

One minister described to me why, after years of trying, he was finally succeeding in reaching young people in his town. He'd stumbled accidently onto something which was working. He started out just going into the local secondary school, and sitting with some of the teenagers from his church during their lunch break. To his surprise, a growing number of other students soon began to take an interest in these midday rap sessions. At first they were simply curious to find out just what this outsider was doing on campus. As weeks went by, though, they began to open up to him and he was able to provide a listening ear for teenagers who would never have darkened the doorstep of his church.

He was learning about youth and, at the same time, sharing with them his faith in Christ.

Jesus always ensured that his message was being heard and understood, not just by a religiously literate minority, but by the widest possible cross-section of the community. If the modern Church is to attract the attention of young people, it will need to take the same approach.

Be Challenging

Many teenagers and young adults see the church as being boring. I suppose that this is due in part to the media's representations of the church and its leaders, not to mention Christ. How often have we seen Jesus represented in the movies as a thin, pathetic-looking figure, who only rarely summons up the energy to crack a smile? And how many movies and TV shows have we seen which feature church leaders and preachers only as charlatans or wimps?

In fact, the Jesus of the gospels was anything but a weak and uninspiring man. Some of the biggest world-changers in history have been churchmen and women who stood bravely against the status quo, often with everything they possessed. Despite their great sacrifices, they showed an uncommon degree of the joy of life. All in the name of the Jesus they sought to imitate.

I remember hearing a religious programme on my car radio one evening. The guest on the show was supposed to be an expert on the life of Christ. When asked if Jesus was a happy person, he replied: 'Well, both history and tradition tell us that Jesus of Nazareth did not smile or laugh a great deal. There seems little in the gospels to suggest that He was a happy person as we know happiness. In fact, we are told in the scriptures that He was perhaps more disposed to weeping.'

I don't think that man has ever really read his Bible! Jesus felt the pain of injustice and the anguish of human suffering more than any other man. But to say that Jesus did not know how to laugh is ignorance. Think about it: If you were able to do the kinds of things Jesus was always doing for others, don't you think you might get a little excited about life now and then? If you could heal the blind, the lame, the deaf, the dumb and even the leper, wouldn't you wear a smile every now and then? No, the real Jesus of history was not a dull man. He enjoyed doing what his Father had given Him to do. He was full of the joy of life.

The way Jesus lived was anything but boring. If He was here today, He would call the young to reach out to the marginalised and unpopular in our society. He would demand, for example, that they take a practical interest in the plight of the elderly, who constitute one of our most forgotten people groups. Studies have shown that 20% of elderly people in the Australian community have no close friends, and that one in five elderly women take sleeping tablets not prescribed by doctors, to help them deal with boredom and loneliness.[1]

Jesus would stir teenagers to action in helping members of ethnic minorities. He would challenge them to visit prisoners, assist widows and care for AIDS and cancer sufferers. He would teach them to pray for the sick and comfort the grieving. In short, Jesus would call kids to stand against the status quo, to live bravely, to rebel in the face of injustice and apathy. He would have them reach out for God's supernatural power in the face of the sickness and spiritual oppression afflicting men and women around them.

More than ever before, today's kids need to see a

Church which teaches and practises the heroics of Christ-like living. Paraphrasing the words of a sage, I would say that: 'The greatest witness to the young is a life—and a Church—which cannot be explained unless there is a God.'

Be Merciful

When my father was a young man, some members of his church considered that young men only grew beards to express rebellion against authority figures. Incredible though it now seems, the growing of beards was frowned upon by some good church people. So was going to a football match and visiting a cinema. Playing cards and snooker were also out because of their associations with gambling.

These are examples of petty man-made rules being imposed over truly biblical principles. They reflect a fear on the part of the Church about the influence the wider world might have upon its young people. Legalism is always the defensive response of an insecure church to a world it does not understand. Legalistic Christianity trivialises the important and emphasises the insignificant.

It is also the very antithesis of the biblical idea of grace. The concept of grace is founded upon the fact that, without God's intervention mankind is lost, morally and spiritually. The sinfulness of the human heart always seems to bring mankind down, no matter how lofty are our intentions. With the apostle Paul, we might complain that: 'The good things that I want to do, I do not; and the evil things which I do not want to do, those are the things I find myself doing' (Romans 7:19).

In its fallen state, human kind is separated from all that a loving God had planned for it, and suffers the outcome of its rebellion against His principles for life. Human beings cannot restore their relationship with God by their own efforts. No amount of good works will do it. Unless God intervenes, mankind is lost forever.

According to the Bible, God has come to our rescue— He has made a way for us to be restored. Through the subsitutionary death of His Son, Jesus Christ, God has dealt with the consequences of our rebellion, and will now heal all who call upon Him. We do not deserve that such a great sacrifice should be made on our behalf, but God has acted in unselfish love. Rather than deal with us according to what we deserve, God has dealt with us according to His mercy. This is grace—God's unmerited favour.

What grace gives us freely, legalism would have us work for and struggle to achieve. I like to illustrate it this way: Suppose an athlete is capable of clearing a high jump bar set at five feet. If the bar is placed any higher than that, the athlete knows that it is beyond him, or her, to make it.

Now suppose the jumper represents someone who wants to find God, and the bar is the only thing which stands between that person and the object of his or her search. In despair, this individual realises that God's standards are too lofty and cries out in frustration.

Suppose then that God reaches down and lifts that person over the bar, without any effort at all on his or her part. What a relief it is to the heavy heart to know that it is now relieved of guilt and every barrier to fellowship is broken down. This is divine grace in operation.

A short while later, however, another lost man or woman approaches the bar. Without compassion the first jumper turns to raise the bar by a further three feet!

The extra three foot space represents a whole host of man-made do's and don'ts, which have nothing to do with God at all. The first athlete says: 'OK, jump. Go on, you can do it. I did!' This is legalism at work.

The Church ought to be giving the world a true picture of the nature and character of God. When it becomes legalistic, the Church offers only a twisted caricature of the Lord and his ways.

For some Christians, the line between true and desirable holiness, and unwanted legalism, has become blurred. Holiness teaches and maintains the right standard, not some arbitrary requirement which has no basis in the Bible. Holiness also has compassion for those who have fallen, while legalism cares only that a rule has been broken. When a woman caught in the very act of adultery is brought before Jesus, He tells her to go her way and 'sin no more.' He does not excuse her sin, but refuses to condemn her as a person in the manner of the Pharisees, who were about to stone her to death. They cared only for the law, Jesus for both the law and the person.

Today, few churchgoers would have a problem with a young man growing a beard. Yet in some quarters, guys who wear earrings are thought rebellious. Even if there were some link between earrings and anti-authoritarian attitudes, a true follower of Christ would be more concerned about the man's inner problem, than with his choice of fashion accessories.

Legalism still exists in some parts of the Church, perhaps it always will. But if we are to reach out to young people in our communities, we must avoid it like the plague that it is. It is heartless, unjust and ungodly.

Be Accessible

One last thing remains to be said about the way teenagers in our society see the Church. Many of them think Christians are, for the most part, hypocritical. To their way of thinking, church services are nothing more than 'tupperware parties'—a lot of hollow plastic people getting together to flip their lids.

One way in which the modern Church can demonstrate its sincerity is by promoting the unique sense of family it can engender among its members. One of the greatest assets the Church has to offer, in a world bereft of meaningful relationships, is its capacity to bring people into caring networks.

I doubt that young people need any more rock stars—there are plenty of those around already. What they do need, and what local churches can provide, are family relationships, fathers and mothers, brothers and sisters. Families are a resource in short supply today.

Jesus said: 'No-one who has left home or brothers or sisters or mother or father or children or fields for me and the gospel will fail to receive a hundred times as much in this age—homes, brothers, sisters, mothers, children and fields . . . ' (Mark 10: 30). Jesus knew that in His Church, people would be able to develop new relationships. New 'families' would be formed as the people of God reached out in His love.

In the last letter he ever wrote, St. Paul admonished his beloved apprentice Timothy with these words: 'The things you have heard me say in the presence of many witnesses, entrust to reliable men who will also be qualified to teach others' (2 Timothy 2:2). Paul, the great missionary of the first century Church, knew that he was about to die for the cause dearest to his heart, the message of Christ's love. Rome was rounding up

Christians and putting them to death in all manner of gruesome ways. Paul knew this might be his last chance to ensure that Timothy had learned the right priorities. One of those priorities was to be fathering others in the faith.

Many older men and women in the Church, and in the community at large, feel a deep concern for the plight of young people, but feel powerless to help them. In many cases, where their own children have grown up and left the nest, they wonder whether they still have anything to contribute.

In fact, older people have a great deal to offer the young. I have found that, in today's environment, what we call 'common sense' is not all that common. Due to the breakdown of extended families, young people are being deprived of valuable opportunites to learn life skills from their elders. Concerned older people can help teenagers and young adults to develop the skills they have acquired through their various experiences in life.

To 'father' or 'mother' the young in this way, however, people must be prepared to throw their lives open, to become accessible to youth. It's of no use us saying to a young person, 'I care about you; let's get to know each other,' if the relationship can only develop on our terms. We will need to bend a little, to accommodate the rough edges of youth. We may need to give of our time, energy and wisdom when it is not convenient or comfortable for us to do so.

I think you would be hard pressed to find a finer example of this kind of accessibility than Jesus Christ. At times, Jesus would have His brothers and sisters, and His disciples, all travelling with Him in one entourage (John 2:12). Most of us, if we wanted to model healthy attitudes for our friends, would not want to get our families involved. For many of us, the home is the hardest place to be on our best behaviour! Jesus was vulnerable with those He wanted to train. He gave of Himself, openly and honestly.

I am not suggesting that we surrender our privacy completely. Far from it. Unless we learn to hide ourselves away sometimes, attending to our marriage or family relationships, and other interests, we will have nothing in reserve to offer others when we are with them. When you become 'stressed out', there's very little that anyone can learn from you—not much that's positive, anyway. Yet, with proper organisation of your time, you may just be able to offer a young person what very few others can (or want to): a father's guidance or a mother's concern.

The Church Has Much To Offer

The Church has a great opportunity to attract and help young people, as it learns to relate to a contemporary generation, both in the style and substance of its message. It must work against common stereotypes, which paint churches as havens for the lifeless and the weak. It needs to place people above long-held traditions, stepping boldly away from serving trivial, man-made regulations, and placing itself in positions where compassion can find practical outlets of service. And, finally, it must learn to place a high premium on relationships—particularly on the local level—fostering the kinds of family networks of which so many young people have been deprived.

Moving Ahead ...

So often parents, youth workers and concerned friends feel inadequate in understanding young people, their subculture and their particular problems. Even more often they are unaware that the pressures and difficulties youth are going through are leading them, in many instances, into deep depression and, worse still, suicide.

Troubled youth, on their part, have not been taught how to handle life's problems, peer pressures and 'fast lane' temptations. Nor do they know how to develop meaningful, lasting relationships. Many lack solid role models to whom they can turn for understanding, guidance, love and encouragement.

I have tried, over the past 16 chapters, to bring the issues faced by young people today into sharp focus.

I have endeavoured to encourage you in your efforts to reach out to youth; to give you confidence in knowing how to begin to help them. I do not have all the answers. Like you, I am constantly learning, discovering and experimenting. I do know, though, that with God's help you and I can offer invaluable, and sometimes life-saving, assistance to young people.

As we reach deep into our reserves of compassion, mercy and generosity of spirit we can pull youth from the flames of despair, inadequacy and anger. We can save this 'endangered species', healing broken hearts and enriching empty lives with the grace and acceptance which God has shown to us through His Son, Jesus Christ. May God equip us and give us His heart for the youth of the '90s.

Part Three

The Rescue Pack

17
The Danger Zone

Warning Signs

There are ways in which we can help deeply depressed young people, bringing them back from the brink of disaster. Recognising the warning signs and treating them seriously is the first step.

Sometimes a young person's depression is overlooked because forms of behaviour which signal depression are not recognised. Some of the major signs which might indicate major depression (and which sometimes, though not always, point toward suicidal thoughts) are listed below:

1. Major Changes in Normal Behaviour
A normally outgoing young person who suddenly becomes sullen and uncommunicative may be signalling depression. A good student who begins to fail at school may also be showing he or she is upset.

2. Sleeping Problems
Depression can sometimes cause young people to sleep at odd hours, becoming tired during the day and overactive and unable to rest at night.

3. Changed Eating Patterns
Excessive dieting or overeating may also mask deep-seated hurts or traumas.

4. Apathy and Lack of Energy
A young man or woman who suddenly seems to have lost interest in life, particularly in things which used to stimulate his or her interest, may be suffering an underlying loss of purpose.

5. Unexpected Cheerfulness after a Long Depression
This may indicate that the person has given up on his or her problems, opting for some more drastic solution.

6. Aggression
Some young people express their pain by throwing temper tantrums and lashing out with physical or verbal violence at the slightest provocation.

7. Risk-Taking Behaviour
Teenagers may show a sense of desperation by getting into fights or taking other unusual risks (eg. playing 'chicken' along train tracks or 'surfing' on top of a moving train).

8. Promiscuity
Sexual promiscuity can be, especially among girls, a way of saying 'I need affection and a reason to live.'

9. Truanting and the Use of Drugs
These forms of behaviour can be a teenager's way of saying, 'If you care, you'll stop me.' Many young people who actually attempt suicide have ambivalent feelings about it. Their actions may be a way of gauging whether

others think they are worth preserving.

10. Neglect of Appearance
This may reflect low self-esteem and a sense of unworthiness, particularly when the person allows his or her appearance to degenerate in a short space of time.

11. Frequent Crying
This may show that a young person is no longer able to cope with his or her situation.

12. Self-Destructive Talk
Suicidal thoughts may be indicated in quite an overt fashion by expressions such as: 'Well, you won't need to worry about me for much longer!' or 'I wish I could go to sleep and never wake up!' or 'They'll be sorry when I'm gone.' Expressions such as these should never be treated lightly.

How Family And Friends Can Help
Depressed, frustrated or despairing young people have great problems on their hands. However, if they have caring family members and friends who see their predicament and genuinely want to help, they are ten times better off than so many thousands of others for whom nobody seems to care!

You may have a child, brother, sister or friend who is displaying some of the danger signals mentioned in the last section. They may be sullen, withdrawn and generally uncommunicative about their problems. There is still hope! You can still reach them. Please don't give in to their despair! Here are a few practical do's and don't's which will help you:

1. Be Observant

Take note of any major changes in the person's behaviour. Children and young adults are particularly vulnerable to major depression during times of upheaval in their circumstances. There may have been a death in the family, or among friends. There may be fights occurring in the family or the family may be moving home (again). The break-up of a close relationship, particularly a boy-girl relationship, can trigger or add significantly to a depressed state.

Trust your instincts if you suspect that someone is suicidal.

2. Be A Good Listener

Try to get the person talking about their problem. This is not always easy, especially if the individual is very depressed and withdrawn, but you can try to open the lines of commmunication by saying something like: 'I've noticed you haven't been quite yourself lately. Can I help?'

If a person does open up and confides in you that he or she is thinking about drastic measures, try to determine how serious is the plan they are forming, and try to remain calm.

Don't trivialise the problem by saying things like: 'Oh, things aren't as bad as all that! That's just a small problem really.'

Don't act in a judgemental way or look or sound shocked by what the person tells you (even if you are!) Try to be constructive with what you say. Ask questions such as: 'Have you thought about suicide before? What stopped you? What was it that made you want to live on?'

As the person responds to your concerned questions,

rephrase his or her responses and feed them back in your words, thus demonstrating your desire to really understand the problem, and allowing your friend to fill in any gaps in your understanding. This also gives the depressed person an important opportunity to hear his or her own attitudes and reasoning expressed by someone else; to order their thinking and follow their thoughts through to logical conclusions. Thank the person for trusting you and having had the courage to talk.

3. Try To Help Them Take A More Positive Approach
If you have gained the confidence of your troubled friends, if they have shared their intentions, try to help them solve the simpler aspects of their problems first (without treating their difficulty as simplistic!) Help them to see that there are simpler solutions than taking their lives; that this is not in fact a solution at all. It leaves the whole situation unresolved. It also leaves behind a trail of new problems for others and, worst of all, wastes a life.

Point out that, while problems are temporary—they will eventually work out, or at least become manageable —suicide is permanent. I vividly remember watching a one-man play which featured a young teenager in a state between time and eternity, immediately after he had committed suicide. He is talking to an unseen figure, the personification of death. He is explaining why what he just did was the most noble thing to do, why he had no other choice. It was his way, he says, of sending a lasting message to all those who had hurt him. After several minutes of this angry and frustrated outburst, he stops, having run out of things to say. There is a pregnant pause. Finally, in a subdued and sober tone of voice, he says: 'By the way, can you tell me how to get back?' The silence that follows is chilling! There can be no way back from suicide.

4. Remove All Lethal Weapons And Potentially Lethal Drugs From The House

How often have we read of suicides where the final disconnection from life, the ultimate act of violence, was made more attractive by the fact that the means were within easy reach? Don't give a severely depressed young person the benefit of the doubt when it comes to sleeping pills, other powerful drugs, or weapons which could be used on themselves.

5. Don't Leave Them Alone Too Much

When young people are known to be extremely troubled and have indicated a morbid fascination for death or escape, it is a serious mistake to leave them alone with too much unoccupied time on their hands. Try to get them involved in outside activites, even small ones such as creating something—cooking, car repairs and the like— or some other constructive pastime. This can sometimes be very difficult, as they may prove unwilling to cooperate, choosing to remain withdrawn. At least you can ensure that there is someone else around them most of the time. It is, of course, impossible to keep a 24 hour vigil, but do your best. Be creative in ensuring that they are within easy reach.

6. Seek Outside Help

I was speaking to a group of senior high school students on the subject of suicide recently, when one of them asked the following question: 'If someone really wants to kill themselves, why not let them do it? It's their life!'

I can give two very good reasons why trying to save a

life is worth it. First of all, there are tens of thousands of people in this nation who can attest to the fact that problems which seem insurmountable today may become manageable tomorrow. What I am a victim of today, I may become victor over tomorrow, with help. Many people who once seriously contemplated or even attempted suicide have gone on to live productive, fulfilling lives.

Secondly, hell on earth is not hell at all. We must each give account one day for what we have done with the gift of life. Our creator will seek an explanation for our actions, thoughts and motivations. Our conscious existence does not end at death. Suicide does not solve our problems. It may, in fact, opens up new ones.

God is merciful. The Bible is clear that He does not want anyone to perish, but to turn and let Him lovingly turn the ship of life around. Nevertheless, the power of choice —etemal life spent in the presence of God, or eternal misery without His presence—remains our God-given prerogative. Reluctantly, but justly, He will honour a person's choice even though it breaks His Father's heart to do so!

There are times in our lives on earth when we must interfere in the affairs of another human being, if it means saving him or her from making a dreadful mistake. We cannot make our children's decisions for them, ultimately the choice for life is still theirs alone. But we must put up a fight, even when they may have given up. We must interfere!

Think about this: if a loved one were to take their own life and you did nothing to help them, even against their wishes, could you easily live with that?

Encourage hurting friends to seek professional help. Don't be ashamed to refer them to someone who is more qualified to help them than you are. Suggest that they talk to a pastor, a trusted teacher, a doctor or suicide prevention worker. Ask them if there is anyone they already know and trust whom they would be prepared to talk openly with. Otherwise, seek help on their behalf, even if they don't ask for it. It may save precious lives!

Part Four

Help Yourself To A Better Relationship

18

Communication Exercises

These next few pages are designed to help you in your communication with your parents (if you're a young person) or your teenage children (if you're a parent).

Communication always begins with listening. The commitment to hear how the other person views a problem is an integral part of all communication between human beings. Sadly, many parents and their children have never learned the discipline of empathising —listening in order to understand.

I hope that, as you and your teenager/parent work through these simple exercises, each of you will discover things about the other which you had previously overlooked. No relationship happens without hard work, so it's worth the time to answer some questions.

Stop . . . Don't Go Any Further!
Please take note of the following pointers before you try any of the exercises which follow:

1. *Choose The Exercise Which Is Most Needful For You Now.* Tackle areas which are most pressing in your relationship. Unless you work on things which really relate to you now, you'll lose motivation and miss the rewards.

2. *The Questions Provided Are Not Part Of An Exam.* Don't be put off by the question-answer format. There are no right or wrong answers, only honest ones. Please be as open as you can. Relationships are built on vulnerability—the commitment to tell it like it is.

3. *Answer The Questions Separately, Then Discuss Them Together.* Parent, if you're the one initiating this process, don't rush your child into answering. Allow a few days for the exercise to be completed individually and set a time for discussion at the end.

4. *When You Come Together For Discussion, Hear Each Other Out.* Don't stifle conversation by condemning the other person's ideas out of hand. Remember, the aim of the exercise is to hear one another's point of view. Work through the questions in any exercise one at a time, taking time to hear what each of you wrote in response. Try to elaborate on what you may have written down, so that you really share your heart.

5. *Make Fresh Commitments To Action.* These exercises are aimed at getting you talking, and acting to build a better relationship. Don't leave any of the exercises open-ended. Make commitments to do something practical about what you have learned—something which will improve your relationship. Make commitments which you can start carrying out immediately—it's too easy to give vague, long-term assurances.

6. *Go For It!*

1. CONFLICT—*Parent Page*

Answer the following questions openly and honestly. The effectiveness of this exercise depends totally on your willingness to 'call it as you see it':

1. List the 2 or 3 things about your teenager(s) which you find most difficult to deal with:

....
....
....

2. Describe how each of these things makes you feel (Deal with each problem area separately, describing what emotions you feel):

....
....
....

3. What changes does your teenager(s) need to make before you will start to feel better about each of these? (Be specific, taking the problem areas one at a time):

....
....
....

4 Can you think of reasons why making these changes might be difficult for him/her/them?

....
....
....

5. List some of the things you value most about your teenager(s):

....
....
....

6. Describe how each of these makes you feel (again, be specific about your emotional responses):

....
....
....

7. List 2 or 3 things about you which your teenager(s) might find difficult to deal with:

....
....
....

8. How can you help him/her/them to feel better about these things? (Make some specific suggestions):

....
....
....

1. CONFLICT—*Teenage Page*
Answer the following questions openly and honestly. This is not an exam! Just 'call it as you see it':
1. List the 2 or 3 things about your parent(s) which you find most difficult to deal with:

....
....
....

2. Describe how each of these things makes you feel (Deal with each problem area separately, describing what emotions you feel):

....
....
....

3. What changes must your parent(s) make before you will start to feel better about each of these? (Be specific, taking the problem areas one at a time):

....

....

....

4. Can you think of reasons why making these changes might be difficult for him/her/them?

....

....

....

5. List some of the things you value most about your parent(s):

....

....

....

6. Describe how each of these makes you feel (again, be specific about your emotions):

....

....

....

7. List 2 or 3 things about you which you think your parent(s) might find difficult to deal with:

....

....

....

8. How can you help your parent(s) to feel better about these things? (Make some specific suggestions):

....

....

....

2. SELF-ESTEEM—*Parent Page 1.*

List 2 or 3 nicknames you were given as a child or teenager:

....

....

....

2. Describe how each of these 'name-tags' made you feel (Be honest about your emotions):

....

....

....

3. Listed below are three key building blocks for a good self-esteem. Write next to each one what you think it means, in your own words:

a) Belonging: ....

....

b) Competence: ....

....

c) Worthiness: ....

....

4. Which one of these three do you think your teenager(s) might have most problems with and which one do you think he/she/they might find comes most naturally to him/her/them?

....

....

....

5. List a few things which happened to you as a child, teenager or young adult which made you feel good about yourself:

....

....

....

6. List a couple of things you might be able to do to help your teenager(s) develop a healthy self-esteem (What can you do to help yourself feel good about you? What could your friends and parents do to help?):

2. SELF-ESTEEM—*Teenage Page*

1. List 2 or 3 nicknames that you've been given either at home or at school:

....
....
....

2. Describe how each of these 'name-tags' makes you feel (be honest about your emotions):

....
....
....

3. Listed below are three key building blocks for a good self-esteem. Write next to each one what you think it means, in your own words:

a) Belonging: ....
....

b) Competence: ....
....

c) Worthiness: ....
....

4. Which one of these three do you think you have most problems with and which one do you think you find comes most naturally to you?

....
....
....

5. List a few things which you think might improve the way you see yourself (What can you do to help yourself

feel good about yourself? What could your friends and parents do to help?):

....
....
....

3. COMMUNICATION—*Parent Page*
1. List the 2 or 3 things you find most difficult to talk about with your teenager(s)?

....
....
....

2. Describe how you feel when you try to talk about each of these with your teenager(s) (What emotions do you experience?):

....
....
....

3. What changes do you think you could make in order to help you and your teenager(s) discuss each of these issues more openly?

....
....
....

4. What changes do you think your teenager(s) could make?

....
....
....

5. Look back over the six principles shared in chapter 15 for resolving conflict. List which of these you think you and your teenager(s) need to work on first:

....

6. List 2 or 3 things you think your teenager(s) might find most difficult to speak awith you about and describe how you think he/she/they might feel in trying to discuss these issues:

....
....
....

7. What changes can you make to help your teenager(s) speak with you about these things?

....
....
....

3. COMMUNICATION—*Teenage Page*
1. List the 2 or 3 things you find most difficult to talk about with your parent(s)?

....
....
....

2. Describe how you feel when you try to talk about each of these with your parent(s) (what emotions do you experience?)

....
....
....

3. What changes do you think you could make in order to help you and your parent(s) discuss each of these issues more openly?

....
....
....

4. What changes do you think your parent(s) could make?

....
....
....

5. Look back over the six principles shared in chapter 15 for resolving conflict. List which of these you think you and your parent(s) need to work on first:

....
....
....

6. List 2 or 3 things you think your parent(s) might find most difficult to speak with you about and describe how you think he/she/they might feel in trying to discuss them:

....
....
....

7. What changes can you make to help your parent(s) speak with you about these things?

....
....
....

Bibliography

CHAPTER 1

(1) R. Eckersley, *Casualties of Change: The Predicament of Youth in Australia*, 1988, 20.

(2) Ibid.

(3) Ibid., citing G. Ochiltree, 'The Effects of marital disruption on children—an Australian perspective', May 1988.

(4) J. Smith and T. Chambers, *'Psychosomatic Suicide' Report*, Care And Communication Concern, 1989.

(5) R. Eckersley op. cit., 19, citing Dr. D. Edgar in Australian Institute of Family Studies Newsletter, April 1988.

(6) Ibid., 24.

(7) Alvin Toffler, *Future Shock*, Pan Books, 1971.

(8) Jo Webber, 'Incest: If it's happening to you', *Dolly Magazine*, March 1988.

CHAPTER 2

(I) R. Eckersley, *Casualties of Change: The Predicament of Youth in Australia*, 1988, 12.

(2) Ibid.

(3) Susan Hocking, 'Control the television and you control young minds', *The Sunday Mail*, Sept. 11, 1988, quoting Dr. Patricia Edgar.

(4) R, Marks, 'Letters', *TheAge*, October 1989.

(5) Quoted by Leilani Corpus, 'The force behind rock', *The Forerunner*, Maranatha Ministries USA, May 1989.

(6) Dr. Gary North, quoted in *Dungeons and Dragons – Only a Game?*, pamphlet published by Pro-Family Forum, Texas, USA.

(7) Dr. James Dobson and Ted Bundy, 'The Death Row Interview', *Charisma and Christian Life*, April 1989.

(8) T. Cumming, S. Goddard, G. Smith, *20th Century Sex*, Word Books (UK), 1986, 82.

(9) Ibid., 73-74.

CHAPTER 3

(1) R. Eckersley, *Casualties of Change: The Predicament of Youth in Australia*, 1988, 10.

(2) Ibid., 11.

(3) University of California study, reported in *The Australian*, Feb. 12 1988 and March 13 1988.

(4) R. Eckersley, op. cit., 10.

(5) *What your family should know about drugs*, Health Dept. Victoria, 1988.

(6) *Statistics on drug abuse in Australia*, Commonwealth Dept. of Health, 1987.

(7) Ibid.

(8) Quoted by Tom Prior, 'Suicide was final refuge from drugs', *The Sun*, May 13, 1988.

(9) *Sex, Drugs, You and Aids*, Health Dept. Victoria.

CHAPTER 4

(1) R. Eckersley, *Casualties of Change: The Predicament of Youth in Australia*, 1988, 18.

(2) Josh McDowell, *How To Help Your Child Say 'No ' To Sexual Pressure*, Word (UK), 1987, 18.

(3) Quoted by Denise Civelli, 'All we need is love', *Geelong Advertiser*, June 23, 1990.

(4) J. McDowell, op. cit., 19.

(5) Ibid.

(6) Ibid., 10.

(7) Dr. James Dobson, *Romantic Love*, Regal Books, 1989, 38.

(8) Cited, ibid., 39.

(9) Ibid.

(10) J, McDowell, op. cit., 132.

(11) Bruce Wilson, *Can God Survive in Australia?*, Albatross Books, 1983, 177.

(12) Mark Metherall, 'Abortions outnumber births in family planning survey', *The Age*, Jan. 5, 1985.

(13) Ibid.

(14) Peter Haran, 'Shall They Live?', *Australia's New Day*, May 1987.

(15) Stuart Rintoul, 'Zoe, 16, decides school is more vital than her baby', *The Australian*, 1990.

(16) *Abortion The Facts*, Right to Choose Coalition, Richmond Victoria, 1984.

(17) *Australia's New Day*, May 1987, 7-8.

(18) Muriel Reddy, 'The tragedy of AIDS babies', *The Age*, Feb. 25, 1990.

(19) Quoted by Gene Antonio, The AIDS Cover Up?, Ignatius Press, 1987, 12.

(20) Cummings, Goddard, Smith, *20th Century Sex*, Word (UK), 1986, 104.

CHAPTER 5

(I) Quoted by Michele Turner, *Stuck!*, Penguin Books, 1983, 5.

(2) Richard J. Barnet, *The Lean Years*, Abacus Books, 1980, 258.

(3) Ibid.

(4) Michele Turner, op. cit., 7.

(5) Catherine Blakers, *Youth and Society: The Two Transitions*, Australian Council for Educational Research, 1990, 113.

(6) Ibid., 100.

(7) Ibid., 102.

(8) Ibid., 115.

(9) M. Turner, op. cit., 195.

(10) C. Blakers, op. cit., 91.

(11) Ibid., 93.

(12) Ibid.

(13) M, Turner, op. cit., 13.

(14) C. Bladers, op. cit., 110.

(15) Ibid., 111, quoting R. Mears in Australian Family Physician, 1982.

(16) Ibid., 113.

(17) M. Turner, op. cit., 219.

(18) Cited by Phillip Adams, 'Principles in practice to save kids', *TheAustralian*, July 2–3, 1988.

(19) C. Blakers, op. cit., 196.

(20) Ibid., 190-191 .

CHAPTER 6

(1) Ernest Becker, *The Denial of Death*, Free Press, 1973.

(2) Alessandra Stanely, 'Child warriors', *Time, Australia*, April 1,1990.

(3) *Australian Journal of Psychology* 1990.

(4) Cited by Fiona Harari, 'A satisfied nation . . .', *The Age*, April 28, 1988.

(5) Quoted by J. Smith, *Advance Australia Where*, Anzea, 1988, 164.

(6) *TheBulletin*, Dec. 19,1989, quoting Hugh Mackay, *The YoungAustralians*.

(7) 'Grave New World', *Time Australia*, Jan. 18, 1988, quoting R. Eckersley.

(8) Ibid.

(9) Ibid., citing Morgan Research poll, 1983.

CHAPTER 7

(1) Reported on 'Focal Point; Too Young To Die', *ABC-TV*, March 4 1986.

(2) R. Eckersley, *Casualties of Change: The Predicament of Youth in Australia*, 1988, 5.

(3) Ibid.

(4) *Time Australia*, Oct. 20, 1986.

(5) Quoted by Eckersley, op. cit., 38.

(6) Ibid., 34

(7) Quoted by Norman Podhoretz, 'Why teenagers are dying', *The Australian*, March 28, 1987.

CHAPTER 10

(1) Dr. James Dobson, *Preparing For Adolescence*, Regal Books, 1980,16.

(2) Gordon Dalbey, *Healing The Masculine Soul*, Word (UK), 1988, 139–142.

(3) Ashley Montagu, *Touching – The Human Significance of the Skin*, Harper and Row, 1986, 150-151 .

(4) Ibid., 208.

(5) Ibid,, 212.

(6) Ibid.

(7) Quoted, Ibid., 225.

(8) G. Dalbey, op. cit., 111, quoting A. Comiskey, *Desert Stream Newsletter*, 1985.

CHAPTER 12

(1) Quoted by Ray Mossholder, *Marriage Plus: A Manual on Marriage and Home Life*, Mossholder Ministries Inc., 1989.

CHAPTER 13

(1) Lane T. Dennis, *The Letters of Francis Schaeffer*, Kingsway 1986, 106.

(2) Ibid.

(3) William Styron, *Sophie's Choice*, Corgi Books, 1979, 680.

(4) Quoted by Terry Brown, 'It's time for me to die', *The Sun*, Oct. 4,1988.

CHAPTER 14

(1) Bruce Narramore, *Adolescence Is Not An Illness*, Revell, 1980, 106.

(2) Australian National Council On AIDS, advertisement published in *Cleo*, May 1989.

(3) T. Cummings, S. Goddard, G. Smith, *20th Century Sex*, Word (UK), 1986, 22.

(4) Ibid., 77.

(5) Ibid., 22.

(6) Ibid., 26-27.

(7) John Smith, *Advance Australia Where?*, Anzea, 1988, 122-124.

(8) Anthony Campolo, *Partly Right*, Word (UK), 1987, 131.

(9) Bruce Wilson, *Can God Survive In Australia?*, Anzea, 1988, 120.

(10) J. Smith, op. cit., 120.

CHAPTER 15

(1) Richard J. Barnet, *The Lean Years*, Abacus (Sphere Books), 1980, 168.

(2) Brian Hathaway, *Beyond Renewal*, Word Books (UK), 1990,148.

(3) Ibid., 150–151.

CHAPTER 16

(1) Ross Peake, 'Growing old with pain and dignity', *The Age*, Oct. 13, 1990.

GET REAL!

Mal Fletcher

There can be no denying the power of decisions made in our youth. As youth ministry is coming into its own around the globe today, young people are becoming a cornerstone of the church's growth. They're not just the church of tomorrow, but very much the church of today!

The greatest need in churches at present is the need for help in training youth for effective leadership. Many start out with great dreams but sadly, because of inadequate preparation, their fire dies out before it can really be channelled into leadership.

Get Real! is a book for:

YOUTH LEADERS desperately searching for practical resources to make their youth group come alive

YOUNG PEOPLE crying out for down-to-earth teaching

CHURCH LEADERS seeking to understand the youth of today

PARENTS wanting to help their children

Catalogue Number YB 9594   £3.99